Wilshire Boulevard

COMMERCIAL LOS ANGELES 1925–1947

Photographs from the "DICK" WHITTINGTON STUDIO

Compiled by BILL BRADLEY

INTERURBAN PRESS
GLENDALE, CALIFORNIA 1981

COMMERCIAL LOS ANGELES, 1925-1947

© 1981 by Interurbans Publications

First Printing: Spring 1981

ISBN 0-916374-45-9

Printed by G. R. Huttner Lithography
Burbank, California

The Studio

Wayne Whittington, 1942

2.   *Wayne Whittington's office, 1934*

3.

Whittington's studio and home, 1939

4.

5.   *1929*

6.   *1934*

Trav-l Lab

8.

During the period covered by this book, the "Dick" Whittington Studio was the largest and finest photography studio in the Los Angeles area. Thanks to elaborate facilities much admired by the trade, it had the capability to shoot just about anything for just about anybody and its clients included every type of manufacturer or retailer. It also took pictures for insurance companies (to show the scene of an accident), magazines, newspapers and advertising agencies. It was a photographer for the 1932 Olympic Games, held in Los Angeles, and the Air Races of 1933 and 1936, two aviation events held at the Los Angeles Airport.

The studio maintained a high standard of technical performance. One way it felt unique was its ability to solve industrial problems through photography. Or, if a manufacturer wanted to show a product to its best advantage, the Whittington Studio could be counted on to find just the right setting, and just the right lighting and composition for that purpose. By always putting the customer first, it avoided taking pictures that were "arty." Instead, it simply tried to satisfy a customer's needs by illustrating precisely what it was the customer wanted illustrated.

This kind of dedication brought contracts for many local—and some national—establishments, whose individual requirements were as varied as they were prolific. Photographs might be needed to record an event, to publicize the development of a product or to show what the company did. They appeared in every printed media and, in later years, on television.

The Studio's business acumen, moreover, was as good as its job performance. In 57 years, it has never had a losing year.

Founded in 1924 by Wayne Whittington, it took its name from a historical figure who was also the subject of a popular children's story, *Dick Whittington and His Cat.* Dick Whittington was a poor orphan who, in the late 14th century, traded his cat for riches to become a merchant and "thrice Lord Mayor of London." The name inspired the choice of Tudor architecture for the studio and also the use of a cat as its trademark. The trademark appeared everywhere: on stationery, promotional literature, Christmas cards. There were even two porcelain cats at the studio's entrance.

Business began in a garage behind Whittington's house at 3845 Wisconsin Street near USC. It expanded into adjacent properties to become a Tudor garden complex complete with swimming pool for swimwear assignments.

During the late 1930s, the studio experienced its greatest growth and at its peak, employed 27 persons. During this period, it launched a news-picture division. The idea of a newly hired employee who had been a news photographer, the division became an active part of the studio for many years. It took pictures of a feature news nature to supplement the wire services and the photographic departments of local newspapers. Its activity later led to work for *Life* magazine and other national publications and to the establishment of an in-house photo stock library. It also developed the Trav-l Lab, a self-contained processing lab on wheels with a 30-foot extension ladder on top.

During World War II, the loss of personnel due to the draft and the severe rationing of silver and paper left the studio able to do only a fraction of its normal business. To counter this, it made its facilities available to the U.S. government; after some negotiating, the Navy agreed to use them under a contract that lasted some 15 years. For a time, Navy personnel reported as employees and most of the work was directed to the war effort. Despite the inconvenience, the Navy's presence gave the Whittington Studio priority in ordering supplies; as a result, it soon was able to again operate at full capacity.

It did remain, however, unable to serve many longstanding clients. When the War was over, the studio nearly had to start all over again. Moreover, it had another more permanent change to deal with—one that the War had helped to bring about. From the surge in wartime production had come an unprecedented demand for photography. In the development of a multitude of new techniques and materials came specialization. To fill the growing need, many companies found it necessary to establish their own photographic departments. In the years that followed, rather than abate, the number of these in-house units actually multiplied, and the in-house concept grew to become an industry-wide standard. What this did, naturally, was to take business away from the independent studios.

The Whittington Studio determined its most valuable asset to be experience and reduced its staff to the most qualified personnel. From profits made during the War, it built a new facility at 1501 W. Olympic Boulevard, a location it considered central to its clients. In 1958 Wayne Whittington turned the then 12-employee business over to his son, Ed.

The studio today is still friendly with many old clients. It continues to do jobs that supplement the work of in-house departments, particularly those jobs the departments cannot or will not do. There are more problems to solve with photography than ever. What is especially important, though, is that it continues to be a family operation.

Born in 1896, Wayne Whittington apparently inherited his vocational interest from his mother. A painter and an amateur photographer, she went all over California around the turn of the century making glass plate negatives. Wayne was raised near Exposition Park. He attended Manual Arts High School and USC, and then served in the Signal Corps in World War I. In 1918, he married Louise Carter, and soon after began his own business, the Acme Tire Company. Deciding that he wasn't cut out for the tire business, he and Louise left to form the studio—with only a Brownie camera given to him by his mother.

His son, Ed, who later joined the business, was also given a camera as a schoolboy and, like his father, sold Manual Arts High School sports pictures to Los Angeles newspapers. Ed worked at the studio after school to pay for flying lessons and racing-car parts—other interests he inherited from his father. He married his high-school sweetheart, Marie Paschall, in 1941. One year later, they enlisted in the Army. While he was piloting planes in the Pacific, she was in Europe serving as a high-speed radio operator. They had three children, Steven, Mark and Teresa, all of whom spent time working at the studio. Mark decided to stay and plans to continue the business.

What follows in this book is a mere sampling of the studio's work. In many cases, hundreds of photographs were taken for a single client—of which only a few might be represented. Most of these were made available by the Huntington Library and Art Gallery in San Marino, where a portion of the Whittington collection is now housed. The client's name appears above each picture or grouping. If none appears, it means that the picture is from the Studio's stock library.

9.
Young Ed Whittington next to a Douglas World Cruiser, 1924

1925–1926

LOS ANGELES CREAMERY:

10.   *The Creamery's main plant, 1120 Towne Avenue*

11.   *Hollywood branch, 1001 Mansfield Avenue*

12.

THE BROADWAY DEPARTMENT STORE:

13.

14.

15.

THE FRANK MELINE COMPANY:

16.   *"Highland Park Villas"; looking north on Yale Drive from Scofield, Glendale*

THE FRANK MELINE COMPANY:

17.   *"Beverly Hills Heights"*

18.

19.　　　　　　　　　　　　*Grading for "California Riviera"*

20.   *On Wilshire Boulevard near Western Avenue*

21.   *Looking north on Western Avenue toward Sunset Boulevard*

22.　　　　　　　　*Looking east on Wilshire Boulevard at the intersection of Western Avenue*

LOS ANGELES GILHAM COMPANY (Public Relations Firm):

23.   *LOS ANGELES LIMITED at Central Station, Central Avenue foot of 5th Street*

24.

25.

CHEVROLET:

26.

At Hal Roach Studios, Culver City

THE TYPEWRITER SHOP:

28.   *7th and Spring Streets, downtown*

By the 1920s, the Los Angeles Creamery was a major Southern California dairy, producing milk, butter, cheese and ice cream as well as other dairy products. It operated out of four plants, in downtown Los Angeles, Hollywood, Pasadena and Glendale, and advertised that "We deliver to 50,000 homes in time for breakfast every morning."

George E. Platt began the firm in 1884 by delivering milk from the one or two cows he owned at what is today 3rd and Beaudry Streets. Because this was a period of rapid development and rising land values, Platt moved his operation to two other locations before 1890—first to Florence, a community in South Central L.A., then to Boyle Heights in the city's eastern hills. The profits he realized from each sale of land helped him to expand. Business was substantial enough by the early 1900s to justify a three-story bottling and processing plant which, upon completion in 1910, was called the largest and best-equipped facility of its kind on the West Coast.

The Creamery sold its farm in Boyle Heights in 1925 and purchased a 3,000-acre ranch in the San Fernando Valley. In 1928 it merged with Golden State Milk Products of San Francisco; the new company operated 33 factories in California and maintained sales offices in most major cities in the U.S. Eventually it became part of today's Foremost. *[10-12]*

The Broadway in 1926 was a small city of services on nine floors where a customer could find, in addition to merchandise, a circulating library (2¢ a day for a book), a barber shop, a beauty shop, a shoeshine stand, a resident nurse, a post office and a classroom for craft instruction.

The store was established in 1896 by Arthur Letts. Born to a landed English family, Letts spent three years as an apprentice in a dry goods store in England before he emigrated with his brother to Canada. In Toronto he worked at a department store for a while; then he went west to Seattle where he started a retail business of his own. He came to Los Angeles seeking better opportunities and purchased, on good faith, a stock of goods at a bankrupt store at 146 South Spring Street. Unhappy with this location, he put a bid on the Broadway Department Store at 4th and Broadway, which had closed. He secured a loan from the Los Angeles National Bank by convincing the bank president that he could take money out of the stock and still have enough left for business. Under Letts, who insisted on quick turnover, the Broadway prospered. By the turn of the century it ranked among the largest stores on the Pacific Coast. Letts himself became a Los Angeles socialite; he lived at Holmby House, an estate at Franklin and Kenmore Avenues in Hollywood that was famous for its gardens. (They were open to the public on Thursdays.)

In 1906, there were plans to move the Broadway to a new building then going up at 7th and Broadway. Letts signed a 50-year lease on it, but then turned its management over to an employee, John Gillespie Bullock. The new building became the home of another department store—Bullocks.

The Broadway built its own building in 1915 on the same site, 4th and Broadway. Letts died on May 18, 1923. His son, Arthur Letts, Jr., managed the business until he retired in 1926. The Letts family maintained a controlling interest in the company until 1946 when investment brokers took over and named Edward W. Carter executive vice-president. Under Carter the store expanded into the regional chain it is today, with 40 stores in 1980. *[13-15]*

Selling status and not just houses was a feature of Southern California real estate in the 1920s. A leader in this approach was the Frank Meline Company, the developer for tracts near Forest Lawn, in Highland Park, Silver Lake and the West Side of Los Angeles. Calling itself "California's foremost realty organization," it was comparable in stature to Coldwell Banker today. Its main office was downtown at 7th and Hill Streets, on the 3rd floor of the Sun Bldg., and by 1924 it maintained 18 branch offices, including one at the Ambassador Hotel.

There was such a thing as the Meline touch; his developments, even the modest ones, were considered a cut above many of the others in quality. Indeed, not one today has lost any of its original desirability, and that "touch" is still evident.

The company also functioned as a broker—it handled half of the sales in Beverly Hills before 1930, for instance. Furthermore, it was as much a booster for Los Angeles as the Chamber of Commerce or the *Los Angeles Times*. A booklet it published in 1929 called *Los Angeles, the Metropolis of the West*, looked just like the promotional Sunday supplements the Chamber used to distribute to newspapers in the Midwest.

Frank Meline came to Los Angeles from Jacksonville, Illinois, when he was 27. Arriving in 1902, he started out as a window dresser at the Hamburger Department Store (now the May Company). In ten years he advanced to merchandise display manager. He left in 1912 to enter the building business where he became a contractor. Among his projects were the Fifth Church of Christ, Scientist and the Garden Court Apartments in Hollywood.

His building activity led to real estate: in 1919 he formed the Frank Meline Company. Then in 1923 he joined with Alphonzo E. Bell, the developer of Bel-Air, and three others in purchasing 22,000 acres in the Santa Monica Mountains. Hoping to increase the value of the property, the group donated land to the city for an extension of Beverly Boulevard (today's Sunset) and urged the Planning Commission to restrict zoning on property facing the boulevard to residential use, which was done following a referendum. This huge tract, which cost $5,400,000 or $250 an acre, was parceled out among the investors. Meline's company developed Castellammare, near Malibu, the California Riviera (including the Riviera Country Club) and many sections of Brentwood. The lots he sold to buyers were generally of one to two acres and, with mechanical graders not yet in universal use, most of the earth moving was performed by scrapers pulled by teams of mules.

Aside from real estate, Meline was also engaged in the laundry business. In 1915 he formed Laundry Properties, Inc., in Hollywood, a firm which pioneered home delivery in this area (starting, of course, with horse-drawn wagons). The venture was so successful that other laundries were opened, including one in Beverly Hills. There were plans in 1928 to build a 12-story building for the Hollywood concern, but they never materialized.

Frank Meline was on the Board of Harbor Commissioners from 1924 to 1927; he was also a member of the Los Angeles Athletic, Hollywood Athletic and Brentwood Country Clubs, among others. Because of failing health, he sold his real estate company in 1941 to his former general manager.

Frank Meline died in his Brentwood Heights home in 1944 when he was 69. Incidentally, the gardens behind his house were used as a location in the 1934 version of *The Count of Monte Cristo*. [16-19]

Yellow cabs have been in many U.S. cities since the early 1900s when John Hertz, who later developed Hertz Rent-A-Car, started the country's first Yellow Cab Company in Chicago. (He imported the idea from Paris.)

The Los Angeles Yellow Cab Company was established by the Tanner family—the same family who set up the Tanner Gray Line Tours—in 1920. A year earlier, the Tanners had set up Yellow Cab operations in Pasadena, Glendale and Santa Monica. The Los Angeles company was licensed to serve all of Los Angeles plus Burbank, Beverly Hills and El Segundo. The Whittington Studio was sought to take a series of photographs for training purposes, to illustrate safety and personal courtesy.

The company was sold to a San Francisco firm in 1926. In the 1960s it became part of the San Diego-based Westgate Corporation of C. Arnholdt Smith. When the fortunes of Smith, who was a close friend of Richard Nixon, collapsed into bankruptcy in 1976, the Los Angeles Yellow Cab operation ceased. Not until July 1977 were Yellow Cabs seen again on city streets; by then, the court had sold the company to the Golden State Transit Corporation. [20-22]

Until the Union Pacific introduced the streamlined CITY OF LOS ANGELES in the 1930s, the LOS ANGELES LIMITED was the line's premier train between Chicago and Los Angeles. Advertisements in 1926 proclaimed that it made the trip in 48¼ hours. Placed in service on December 17, 1905, the train lasted until the early 1950s. [23-25]

1928–1929

NELSON AND PRICE:

29.   *At the Hollywood branch, 6433 Sunset Boulevard. Next to the balloon is silent screen actress, Mary Brian.*

30.

31. *"India" tires on dairy truck; Adohr Creamery, South La Cienega Boulevard*

32.   *Filling bottles with perfumes and lotions; McCadden Place, Hollywood*

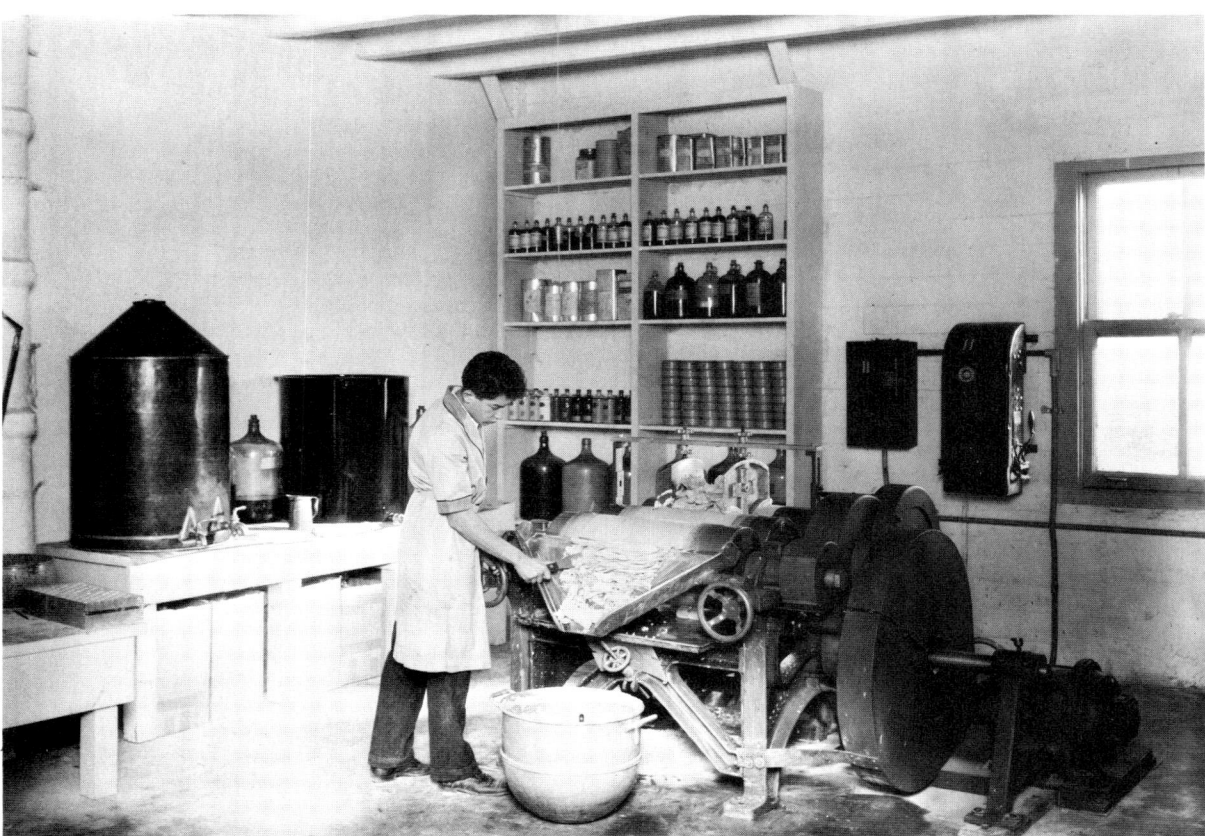

33.   *Making lipstick on a rotor-mill press*

ORIGINAL STAGE LINES:

34.   *At San Fernando Road near Chatsworth Drive, San Fernando*

MUTUAL DAIRY ASSOCIATION:

35.

36.   *Using new double caps with plug and wraparound; 1950 Naomi Avenue (south-central Los Angeles)*

MADDUX AIR LINES:

37. *Exhibit at the National Air Races and Aeronautical Exposition; Mines Field, Inglewood*

MADDUX AIR LINES:

38. *Securities bound for San Francisco*

39.

40. *Lincoln showroom and Maddux headquarters; 2100 South Figueroa Street*

41.   *Inside a Tri-Motor*

MADDUX AIR LINES:

42.　　　　　　　*Mrs. Maddux, Amelia Earhart and Gladys McConnell; Grand Central Airport, Glendale*

DAN BENTON MINER (Publicity):

43.

44.   *"Woodlites" on a Rolls-Royce and a La Salle*

CYCLETOW SERVICE:

45.

THE FRANK MELINE COMPANY:

46.   *At the Riviera Country Club*

P. N. SNYDER:

47.   *Opening Day; Midwick View Estates, Monterey Park, looking toward the fountain and cascade*

HUGH EVANS AND COMPANY (Real Estate):

48.   "Brentwood Riviera"

HAMLIN NERNEY FORD:

49.

50.   *5215 South Vermont Avenue*

MAY COMPANY:

51.

52.

53.   *Movie actress, Sally Blane, at the Dollar Steamship Line; San Pedro*

WHITE MOTOR CORPORATION:

54.   *Buses of the Union Pacific Stage Company; East Los Angeles Station*

Nelson and Price was an independent dealer for both Goodyear "India" tires and U.S. tires. Claiming to be the world's largest retail tire firm, it had, in 1929, 17 branches in Southern California. Founded in 1913 by Frank T. Price, it was an active promoter. As it expanded, it relocated its downtown store and headquarters four times; the last location, at 1323 South Flower Street, opened in July 1929 and was, by today's standards, fairly well appointed with bas-relief and potted palms. Attractive showrooms, in fact, were a company trademark. [29-31]

Max Factor was unique among cosmetics firms because of its close association with Hollywood and the movie industry. Beginning in 1914 when it first supplied motion picture makeup (the first company to do so), the association lasted for about as long as glamour lasted in Hollywood.

Born in Russia, Max Factor, Sr., emigrated to America in 1904. His first business venture was a small concession at the 1904 World's Fair in St. Louis, where he sold perfume, makeup and hairgoods. He and his family moved to Los Angeles four years later and opened a store on Hill Street. On January 2, 1909, Max Factor and Company was officially founded. By 1927 it was distributing its products nationally and by 1930, internationally. Two company milestones were the opening, in 1935, of the unique Max Factor Make-Up Salon in Hollywood, which popularized all types of feminine grooming, and the introduction of Pan-Cake Make-Up in 1937, the forerunner of all modern cake makeup.

In 1958, manufacturing facilities were moved from Hollywood to a new plant on a 13-acre site in Hawthorne. Recently, however, the company announced plans to close this plant and relocate to North Carolina.

Max Factor has been a wholly-owned subsidiary of Norton–Simon, Inc., since 1972. [32, 33]

In 1928, the Original Stage Line ran buses every 30 minutes between Los Angeles and San Fernando on a route along San Fernando Road that is today the 24 Line of the RTD (Southern California Rapid Transit District). The fare to Burbank then was 25¢; to San Fernando, it was 50¢.

Founded in 1913 by W. C. Dunlap, it was one of several bus companies formed to reach areas not served by either the Los Angeles Railway or the Pacific Electric "Red Cars." It was also the first auto stage line to serve the San Fernando Valley from downtown Los Angeles.

Following the 1929 stock market crash, the Twin Coach buses shown in Whittington's picture were repossessed, and the company's ownership changed hands. [34]

Maddux Air Lines was among the many passenger airline companies that were formed in the late 1920s. Its founding was prompted by the introduction of an airplane built by the Ford Motor Company called the Tri-Motor, which featured three engines, all-metal construction and a large carrying capacity.

John L. Maddux had been a Lincoln dealer when he bought a Tri-Motor in 1927. Encouraged by a friend, he put the plane into service between Los Angeles and San Diego on July 21, 1927, with Charles Lindbergh as the pilot. Two months later, the airline was incorporated and, within a year, it had a fleet of eight Tri-Motors. By March 1929, the fleet had been increased to 14 and regularly scheduled service was offered on three routes: Los Angeles–Bakersfield–Fresno–San Francisco; Los Angeles–San Diego–Agua Caliente, Mexico; Los Angeles–Tri-Cities (San Bernardino, Riverside, Colton)–Palm Springs–Imperial–Calexico–Phoenix. The flying time to Phoenix, a distance of more than 400 miles from Los Angeles, was four hours and fifteen minutes. The fare from Los Angeles to San Francisco was $35 one way and $67 round trip. An express flight which left each city at 2:30 P.M. took three hours and cost an extra $3.

Originally based at Rogers Airport (located at Western Avenue and El Segundo Boulevard) Maddux moved its operations to Grand Central Airport in February 1929. In May of that year, it inaugurated a limousine service between the airport and its downtown ticket office at 636 South Olive Street.

Despite a large following among members of the film industry and supplementary income from charter and sightseeing flights, Maddux failed to show much profit without mail contracts, a lucrative business for the early airlines. In November 1929, it merged with Transcontinental Air Transport to become, for a time, TAT–Maddux, with Jack Maddux as president. The new company sought a U.S. mail contract between Los Angeles and Kansas City in competition to Western Air Express, another Los Angeles-based carrier. The Postmaster General refused to grant two contracts on the same route, so the competitors merged to form Transcontinental and Western Air, the parent company to today's Trans World Airlines. [37-42]

Woodlites were invented to solve the problem of headlight glare. Featuring a unique design that focused light through an elongated slit, they were sold as a custom accessory on Packards and other luxury automobiles.

The Woodlite Company also made flood and airport lights; its plant in Hollydale was bought in 1933 by Murray Steel Products of Cleveland, and converted to other uses. [43, 44]

The P. N. Snyder Organization, which had developed property in East Los Angeles, set out with Midwick View Estates to create an exclusive residential and business district for managers of the nearby industrial area. ("Exclusive" then meant a restriction as to race and religion.) The organization purchased 367 acres for $2 million in 1928; it then completed an extension of Atlantic Avenue, paved streets, installed street lights, and hired architects to draw up house plans in Spanish and Mediterranean styles. It also had plans drawn for a recreational system with playgrounds and a 5,000-seat amphitheatre.

The tract received some praise for its visionary planning, but its opening came during a real estate recession followed within months by the Depression. Consequently, few of the lots sold, despite a major promotional effort. However, the fountain and its cascade, planned as the centerpiece of the tract, did survive and are today the trademarks of the city of Monterey Park. [47]

Cycletow Service attempted to use the motor-cycle commercially as a service and delivery vehicle. [45]

The May Company, a department store chain based in St. Louis, entered Los Angeles in 1923 with the acquisition of Hamburger's Department Store. In 1929, it built a nine-story addition to the original building at Broadway and Eighth Streets, which it still occupies. Also in 1929, it proposed to build a new store in Hollywood at the corner of Sunset and Vine. But the Depression caused a change of plans, and the store's first branch was finally built in the Miracle Mile in 1939.

The founder, David May, was a believer in establishing good will between merchant and patron. He died at his home in Beverly Hills in 1927. [51-53]

The White Motor Corporation was a builder of trucks and buses based in Cleveland, Ohio. [54]

The Union Pacific Stage Company was formed by the Union Pacific Railroad in 1927 first to operate tour buses to Death Valley. The intention was to attract more tourists to the line's Overland Route, a route between Chicago and Los Angeles then considered less scenic than that of rival Santa Fe Railroad. Never too successful, the tour operation was ended in 1930. The Stage Company endured, however.

In 1928, Union Pacific decided to replace a costly branch line it operated between Los Angeles and East San Pedro with buses. At the same time, it sought two other routes: Los Angeles–Pasadena–Glendale and Los Angeles–Anaheim. To counter opposition from the Pacific Electric and two bus lines (who feared competition), it had to agree to limit its runs to only those passengers going to and from Union Pacific trains. The railroad built East Los Angeles Station, located six miles from Central Station at Atlantic Blvd. and Telegraph Road to function as a transfer point, much like 125th Street in New York. The Stage Company's three lines inaugurated service on May 15, 1929; they operated with little change until the arrival of Amtrak in 1971.

Today, regular bus service exists only between Los Angeles and Anaheim; the operator is the American Pacific Stage Company.

LOS ANGELES SARATOGA CHIP AND PRETZEL COMPANY:

55.

CURTISS-WRIGHT:

56.   *Grand Central Airport, Glendale*

RICHFIELD:

57.   *Fred Duesenberg and Harry Miller*

MANDARIN FOOD PRODUCTS:

58.

MADDUX LINCOLN:

59.   *Beverly Hills branch*

60.   *Hollywood branch; 1353 North Vine Street*

61.   *Los Angeles Municipal Airport (Mines Field)*

HENRY DE ROULET COMPANY:

62.   *Looking east on Wilshire Boulevard at the intersection of Western Avenue*

Max Ginsberg, a native Pennsylvanian, started the Los Angeles Saratoga Chip and Pretzel Company in 1925. When he sold it 20 years later, his enterprise consisted of 20 production employees at a small plant in Vernon and 10 sales routes that covered most of metropolitan Los Angeles. Under new ownership, the name was changed to Bell Brand Foods, Ltd. The company expanded with new products and territory; in 1968, it became a subsidiary of Sunshine Biscuits. [55]

Grand Central Airport opened on the site of the old Glendale Airport in February 1929. Until the late 1930s it was the area's best-equipped air facility and the most likely point of arrival and departure for anyone traveling by air.

A time when airplanes—or "aeroplanes"—were being taken more seriously as a means of transportation, Grand Central's developers, C.C. and C.A. Spicer, must have recognized the need for a good airport that was suited to passengers. Grand Central became the preferred choice for two of the area's more ambitious lines: Maddux and Transcontinental Air Transport. Late in 1929 it was purchased by Curtiss–Wright, a company based in New Jersey that was preeminent across the country in airport operations, airplane sales and service. It set up a school, the Curtiss–Wright Technical Institute, which was to dominate the airport's activity long after passenger traffic moved elsewhere. The school trained master mechanics for the Air Corps and Navy during World War II; it also produced more mobile training units for the war effort than any other private concern. C.C. Moseley bought the airport from Curtiss-Wright in 1944; he renamed the school Cal-Aero Technical Institute, and he took steps to develop some of the airport's property into an industrial park.

Even in the '50s, Grand Central was a leader in airplane maintenance. But the site was not adequate for the larger planes, or for jets, and in 1959 the runway was closed.

Now owned by the Prudential Insurance Company, it is called the Grand Central Industrial Center. [56]

Harry Miller and Fred Duesenberg were distinguished American auto builders. Miller was especially famous for his development of high-performance engines used in racing cars. Duesenberg also built racing engines, but he became better known as a builder of car chassis. A model he introduced in 1928 is considered by many to be the finest car ever built in America. [57]

Mines Field was one of many airstrips used by Los Angeles area fliers during the 1920s. It gained attention in 1928 when the National Air Races and Aeronautical Exposition was held there. A kind of world's fair of flying with exhibits and stunts by noted aviators, this event attracted more than 200,000 spectators. At its conclusion, the City of Los Angeles took over operation of the field on a 10-year lease. In 1929, the first permanent hangar was built by the Curtiss–Wright Company for a flying school. Later that same year, two more hangars and an administration building were built by the City. In the years that followed, however, the airport attracted little business. Airline companies found its location too remote to attract passengers, and so stayed away. The City, moreover, was unable to fund adequate development to make the field competitive.

This changed as World War II approached. With the help of a federal grant, the City bought the airport; laid down a permanent, paved landing strip, and improved the existing facilities. Late in 1946, the airport became home to TWA, Pan American, United, American and Western Airlines. On May 17, 1950, it was rechristened as Los Angeles International Airport. [61]

Henry de Roulet is best remembered for the Pelissier Building, which he built on the site of his real estate office in 1930. Named for his grandfather, it was built on property that he had inherited from his family. (The property had been a sheep ranch.) The building is historically significant because it set the trend which altered Wilshire Boulevard from a residential to a business thoroughfare. [62]

1931

HATTEM'S MARKET:

63.   *8035 South Vermont Avenue*

64.

65.

SEE'S CANDIES:

66.   *519 West Washington Boulevard, Los Angeles*

67.

68.

WALTER H. LEIMERT COMPANY:

69.   "Terrace Park," Los Angeles

70.   *The sales office at "Terrace Park"—now City Terrace—in East Los Angeles*

Hattem's Market was one of the "sights" in Los Angeles during the 1930s. Self-service counters and an adjacent parking lot also made it something of a prototype of the postwar supermarket.

Actually, there were two Hattem's Markets. The first one, which had a traditional design with red tile roofs and a Spanish-style courtyard, had opened in December 1927 with a two-week celebration that featured free samples, klieg lights, balloons and entertainment from jazz bands, singers, dancers. Its success inspired the second market, which was opened on April 4, 1931. Designed in the Moderne style by Walter R. Hagedohm, its most distinctive feature was a 125-foot-high tower, where the store's creator, Isadore M. Hattem, had his office. Connected by an electrically lit arch to the store was another building that was leased to retailers.

Hattem, who was born in Constantinople, came to Los Angeles in 1913 when he was 19. After working at a downtown fruit stand, he established his own business with two and, later, four stalls at Grand Central Market, following its opening in 1917. This lasted until 1931, when he sold the business to his younger brother, Solomon.

Hattem was remembered as a shrewd grocer with a flair for showmanship. His stores celebrated their anniversaries in a big way with festivities borrowed from opening day and a huge birthday cake that was shared with customers. The stores also offered sales incentives such as their own trading stamps (a filled book was worth $2.50).

For some reason, possibly ailing health, Hattem sold his markets in 1936. The first one was converted to a barbeque restaurant and bowling alley, and later torn down to make way for a bank. The buildings housing the second market became part of Pepperdine University.

Hattem returned to the grocery business in 1944 at the Town and Country Market across from the Farmer's Market. Five years later, he retired to Mexico City, where he died in 1966 at age 72. *[63-65]*

See's Candies completed its manufacturing "studio" in 1931.

Charles See had opened his first candy store in 1921 on Western Avenue. An immigrant from Canada, and originally a pharmacist, he used a portrait of his mother, Mary, as a symbol in the store and on the boxes. This, in addition to the store's decor and management, was consistent with other candy retailers of the period, like Fanny Farmer or the Laura Secord Shops in Canada.

See's Candies survived the Depression by campaigning with landlords for lower rents. It was able, in 1936, to expand into the Bay Area with a new plant in South San Francisco. During the War when materials were scarce, it kept its stores open for shorter periods rather than close altogether or compromise on quality. This often produced long lines, a feature of wartime Los Angeles that many residents remember.

After the War, See's replaced its Los Angeles and San Francisco "studios" with larger facilities.

In this age of the shopping mall, the familiar See's Candy Store remains—by design—almost completely unchanged from the 1920s. *[66-68]*

Before coming to Southern California in 1924, Walter H. Leimert was a major land developer in the city of Oakland, where he was born in 1875. He incorporated his firm, the Walter H. Leimert Co., in 1912. Through it he became known as one of the "Big Four" in East Bay real estate. On occasion he enlisted Jack London to write some ad copy and there is today a Leimert Blvd. named for him.

In Southern California, he first centered his building activity in Glendale. Later developments included: "Terrace Park" (now City Terrace), "Leimert Park" (still known by that name, near Crenshaw and Santa Barbara Streets), part of Cheviot Hills, "Beverlywood" and, following World War II, a portion of Baldwin Hills.

Leimert's son, Walter, Jr., has continued the business. *[69, 70]*

UNIVERSAL AUTO:

71.   *Looking south on Woodman at the intersection of Riverside Drive; San Fernando Valley*

GOLDEN WEST PRODUCTS:

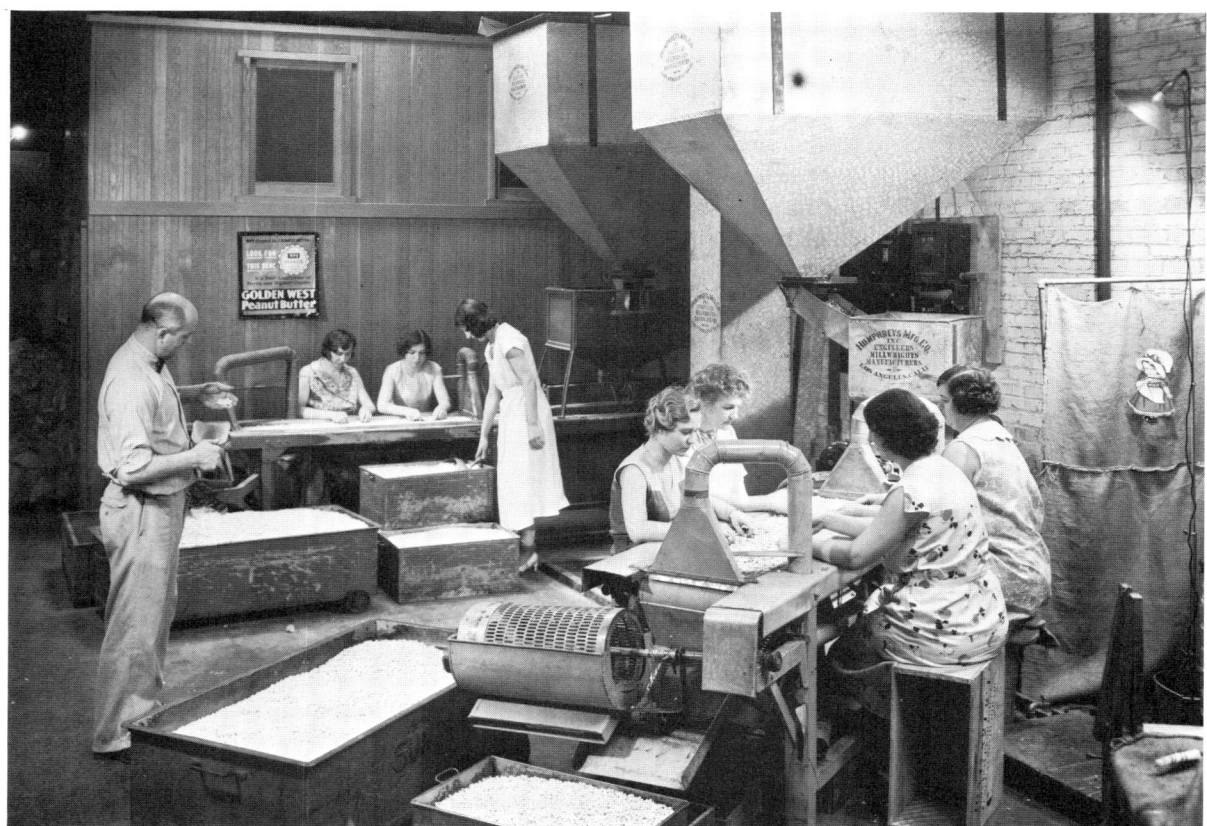

72.

73.   *2465 Hunter*

SOUTHERN CALIFORNIA BUSINESS Magazine:

74.

Assembling the Northrop "Alpha"; Burbank

SIGNAL OIL COMPANY:

75.

Tarzan Club Boat Race; Venice

Golden West Products, Inc., was a manufacturer of peanut butter and salted nuts. Its founding came when peanuts and peanut products were being touted for their nutritional value. The company was 45% owned by Leslie Salt of San Francisco. *[72, 73]*

Signal Oil was spawned from the bonanza of Signal Hill, which, in the 1920s, was the richest oil field per acre in history. Samuel B. Mosher, a citrus farmer from Pico Rivera, formed the company in response to the excess fuel that was either evaporating or being allowed to escape from the drilling operations. He and some associates developed a still that could turn this waste (called "wet gas") into a rich, high grade of gasoline. With the cooperation of the oil companies, he hooked up the still to their lines and started a successful business selling his product to the trade. In 1925, a similar operation was set up in Oklahoma; in 1927, the company entered wholesale gasoline marketing. By then, it had become the largest producer of natural gasoline in the U.S. among companies engaged exclusively in that line. Within five years of its founding, Signal was worth $5 million.

The Signal Oil and Gas Company was founded in 1928 when Mosher started drilling his own oil wells near Bakersfield. This brought the company into the production end of the business, but, ironically, it was the Depression which pushed it into refining and marketing—at a time when other oil companies were cutting back. Signal had been selling its entire output to Standard Oil, but by the end of 1930, Standard declined to renew the contract because of declining sales. With the help of the Bank of America, Signal purchased both a failing refinery in Paramount, California, and a string of moribund filling stations along the California coast. In just weeks, it had designed its famed "Go Sign" trademark (inspired by the unique semaphore traffic signals in the Los Angeles area) and with a cut-rate strategy successfully carved out a satisfying slice of the retail gasoline market on the West Coast.

Always with a flair for the unusual, Signal was an early user of radio to promote its gasoline and in 1932 signed up to sponsor the Tarzan—Ape man—radio program. The company formed "Tarzan Clubs" which enrolled hundreds of thousands of eager youngsters as members, each one of them pestering a parent into trading at a Signal gas station for Tarzan premiums. The club also sponsored intramural contests in a variety of locations. By 1934 the club had enrolled 415,000 boys and girls, and literally destroyed itself as the paperwork burden became too much for the Signal staff at headquarters in Los Angeles.

World War II brought Signal into overseas expansion, especially in the Middle East, and in 1958 the company merged with Hancock Oil and two smaller firms which improved both retailing and refinery capacity. Then came a 1964 merger with the Garrett Corp. and an entry into the aerospace industry.

This development proved to be both an end and a beginning. The company began to divest itself of its production oil activities (its chain of service stations was sold to Exxon) but it invested heavily in other fields, purchasing Mack Trucks, and interests in American President Lines and Golden West Broadcasters. *[75, 76]*

1934

UNION OIL:

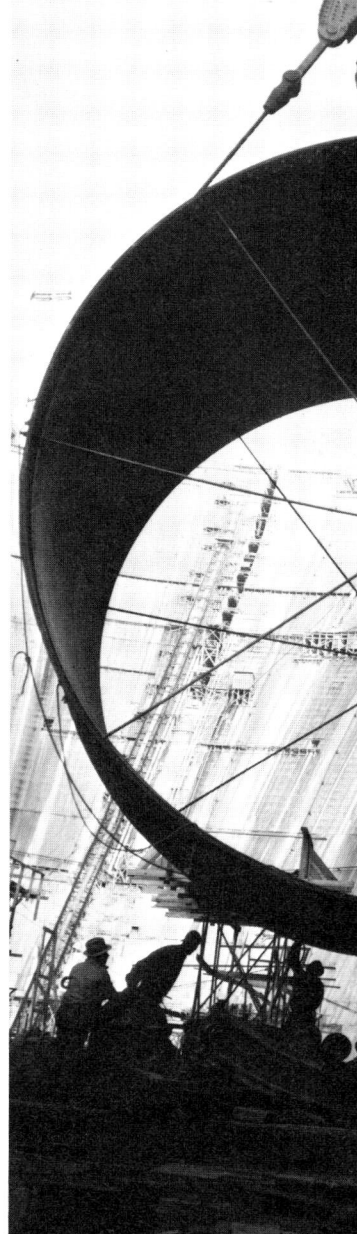

77.   *Boulder Dam under construction*   78.

79.

DRIVE-IN THEATRE:

10860 West Pico Boulevard

WILLIAM SIMPSON CONSTRUCTION:

Griffith Park Observatory and Planetarium

COAST FISHING:

83.   *Packing "Balto" cat food; Terminal Island*

CLAYTON MANUFACTURING COMPANY:

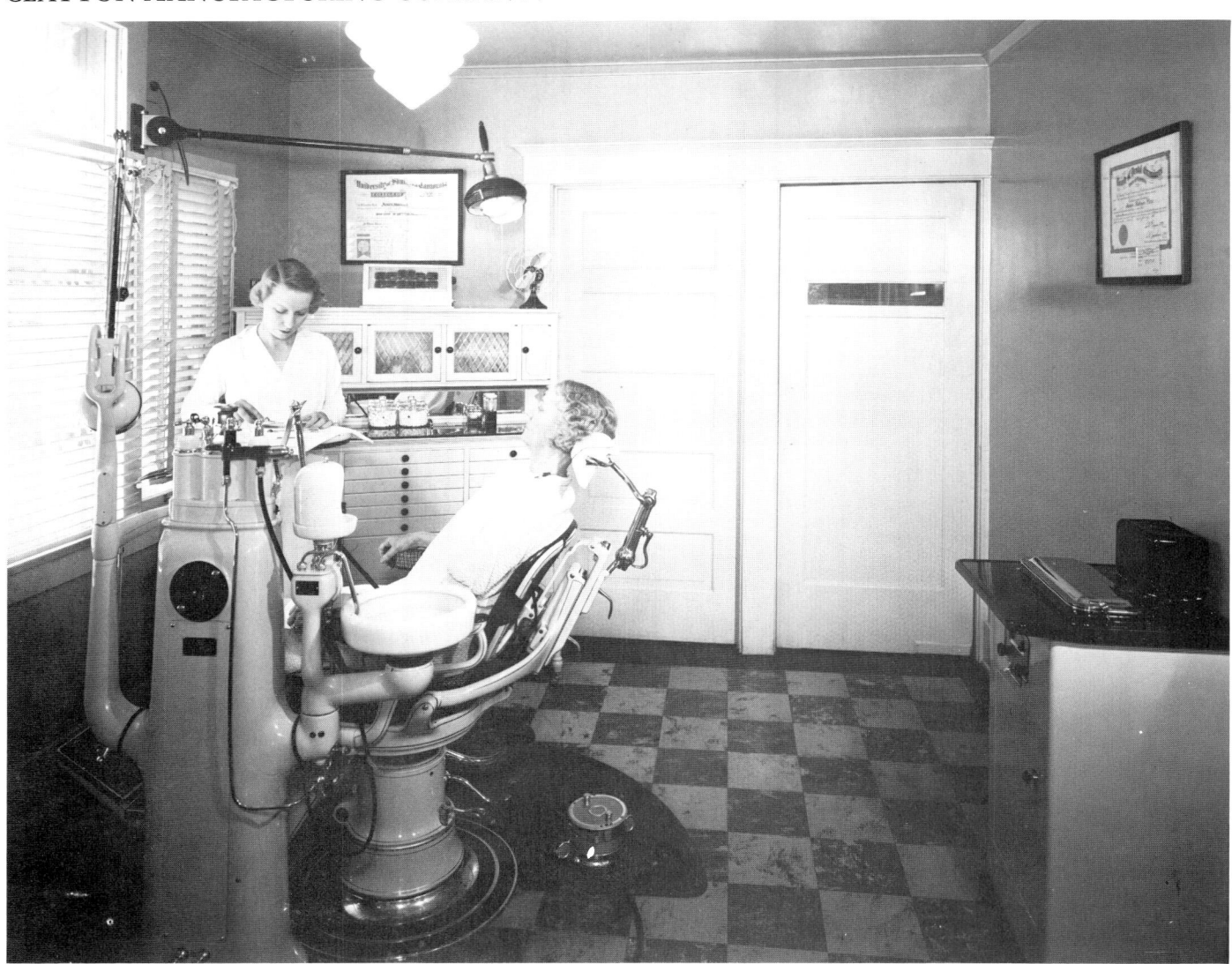

The office of Dr. James Madison Pierce; 4401 Melrose Avenue

EARLE C. ANTHONY:

85.   *Publicity for a Hudson automobile*

PACIFIC OUTDOOR ADVERTISING:

86.

87.

88.

Even though it isn't in California, Boulder Dam (now Hoover Dam) has been a vital part of the Los Angeles area's economy since it was dedicated by Franklin D. Roosevelt on September 30, 1935.

Transmission lines for the City of Los Angeles and independent power companies such as Southern California Edison were put into service, starting in 1937. In 1941, the Metropolitan Water District completed an aqueduct to Los Angeles from an intake point downstream from the Dam. *[77-79]*

William Simpson Construction, a name which is pressed into many sidewalks around Los Angeles, was the contractor for the Griffith Park Observatory and Planetarium, the Emmanuel Presbyterian Church on Wilshire Blvd., the Pantages Theatre in Hollywood, the Beverly Wilshire Hotel, CBS Television City and Occidental Center, among many others.

William M. Simpson started the company in Denver in 1879; he moved it to San Diego in 1900, and to Los Angeles in 1915. His son and grandson—both named William—continued the business following his death in 1917.

In 1968, it became the Simpson Division, Dillingham Construction—a part of the Honolulu-based Dillingham Corporation. *[82]*

It wouldn't take long for any Los Angeles resident of more than 15 years to recognize the one name associated for decades with both automobiles and broadcasting—Earle C. Anthony. It was a case of the best of both worlds: the radio station he owned, KFI, gave his Packard Motor Car distributorship a mention with each station break.

Anthony had a habit of making the news. Born in Washington, Illinois, he came to Los Angeles in 1892 when he was 12. Becoming one of the earliest drivers of a ''horseless carriage,'' he was involved in the city's first recorded traffic accident—in 1897—when his runabout hit a pothole at six miles per hour.

He attended the University of California at Berkeley, where he founded *The Pelican,* a nationally known campus humor magazine. After a year of postgraduate work at Cornell University, Anthony returned to Los Angeles in 1904 and opened an auto dealership, using money he had earned as a part-time newspaper photographer—one of the earliest.

It was in 1922 that Anthony, often playing the part of the pioneer, went into the radio business by acquiring station KFI in Los Angeles. This high-powered station, with its National Broadcasting Co. affiliation, lent further renown to Anthony's efforts. He started a second Los Angeles station, KECA (using his initials), but sold it in 1944 because of a new federal regulation barring ownership of two stations in the same market.

Another one of his pioneering efforts was the opening of one of the first ''service stations'' in Los Angeles at Washington Blvd. and Grand, back in the early days when many automobilists were buying their gasoline at the livery stable.

This station grew into a chain of some 250 along the West Coast, but Anthony sold them to Standard Oil in 1914, thus furnishing the oil giant with ready-made marketing outlets.

In 1956 Anthony sold his estate at 1 Los Feliz Park and moved to Palm Springs; he died in 1961 at age 80. *[85]*

Clayton Manufacturing Company was formed originally to produce and market a single device, the Kerrick Kleaner. Invented by Walter Kerrick in 1929, this was the first mechanical steam cleaner. The firm expanded its line in the 1930s to include cleaning compounds and steam generators. For a short time, it made pneumatic air compressors used in dental offices which were based on principles of the Kerrick Kleaner.

Today, Clayton has its headquarters in El Monte, with branch plants in Belgium and Mexico. *[84]*

Pacific Outdoor Advertising was established by Helen A. Brown in 1930 with the purchase of 15 modest highway signs. It was, and still is, a rival to Foster & Kleiser, also based in Los Angeles, and it now has some 1,300 billboards across the country. *[86-88]*

EARLE C. ANTHONY:

89.   *Old and new Packards; Union Air Terminal, Burbank*

1937–1938

JONATHAN CLUB:

90.   545 South Figueroa Street, Los Angeles

91.

DODSON, LTD.:

92.

CAR AND GENERAL INSURANCE:

93.   Currie's Ice Cream Store; 3701 Beverly Boulevard

CHECKER BARBER SUPPLY:

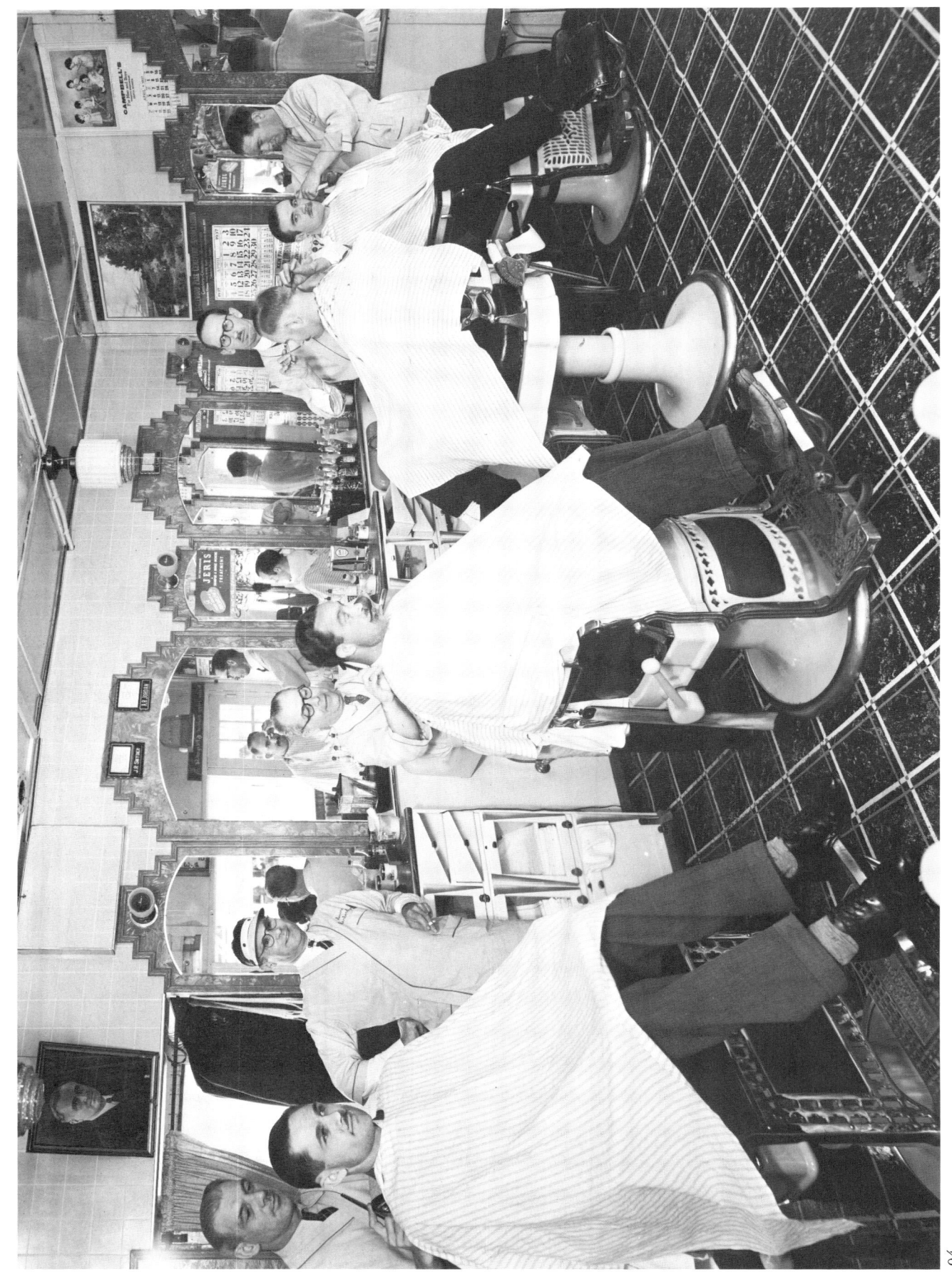

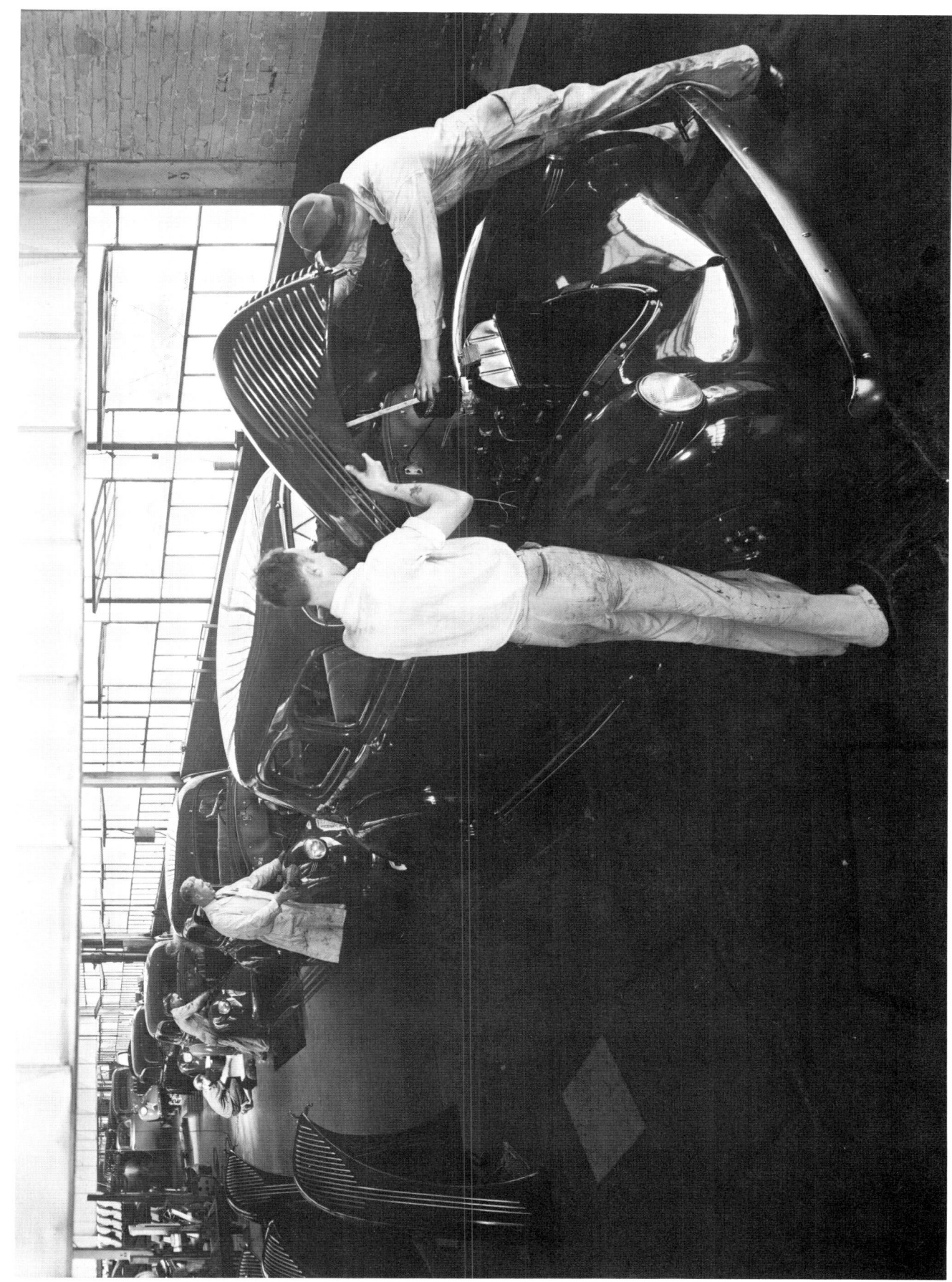

Willys–Overland Plant, Vernon

FORD MOTOR COMPANY:

Grunion party; Huntington Beach. Louise Whittington is standing at the right.

615 South Broadway

LOS ANGELES THEATRE:

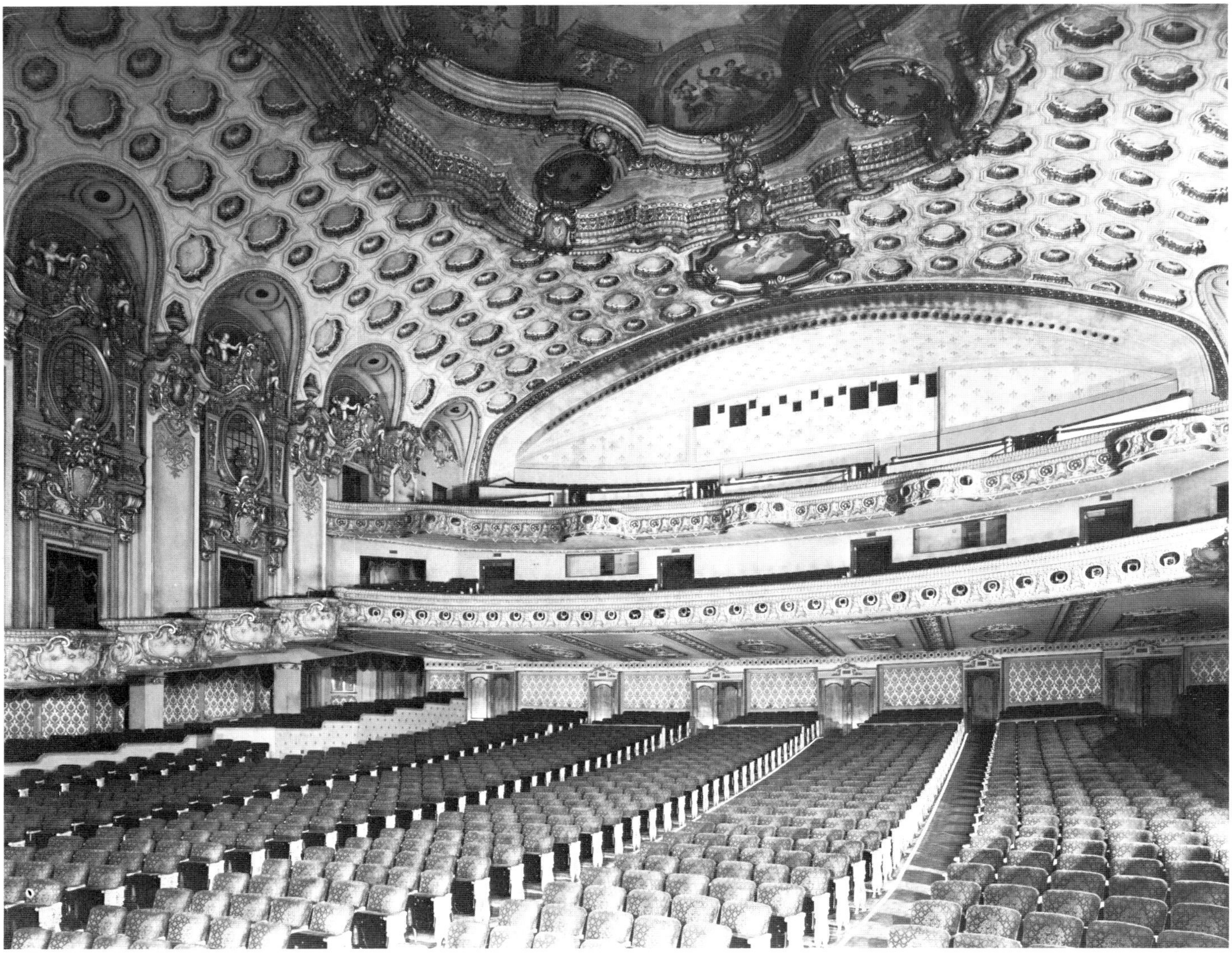

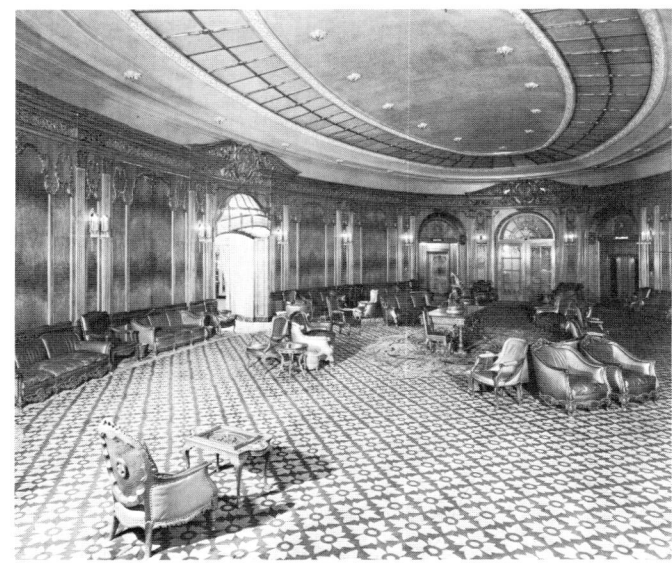

98.

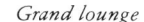

99. *Grand lounge*

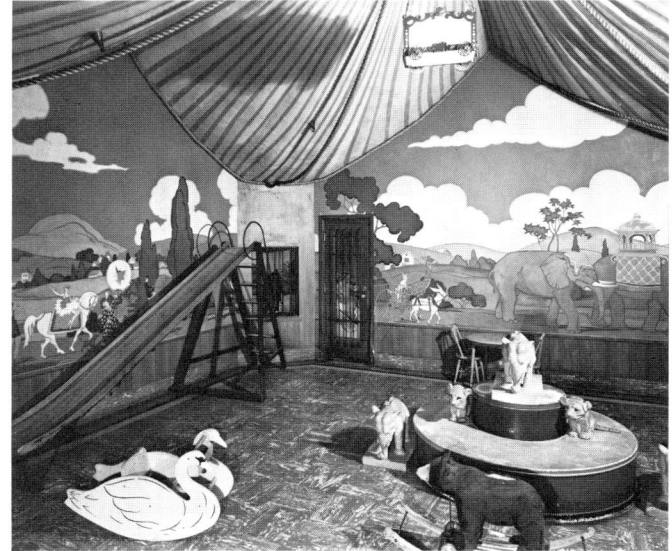

100. *Children's playroom*

Southern California Telephone Building, 740 South Olive

Studebaker Plant, Vernon

103.

Standard Oil Building, 605 West Olympic Boulevard

CALIFORNIA FRUIT GROWERS ASSOCIATION:

San Fernando Heights Packing House

VAN DE KAMP'S HOLLAND DUTCH BAKERS:

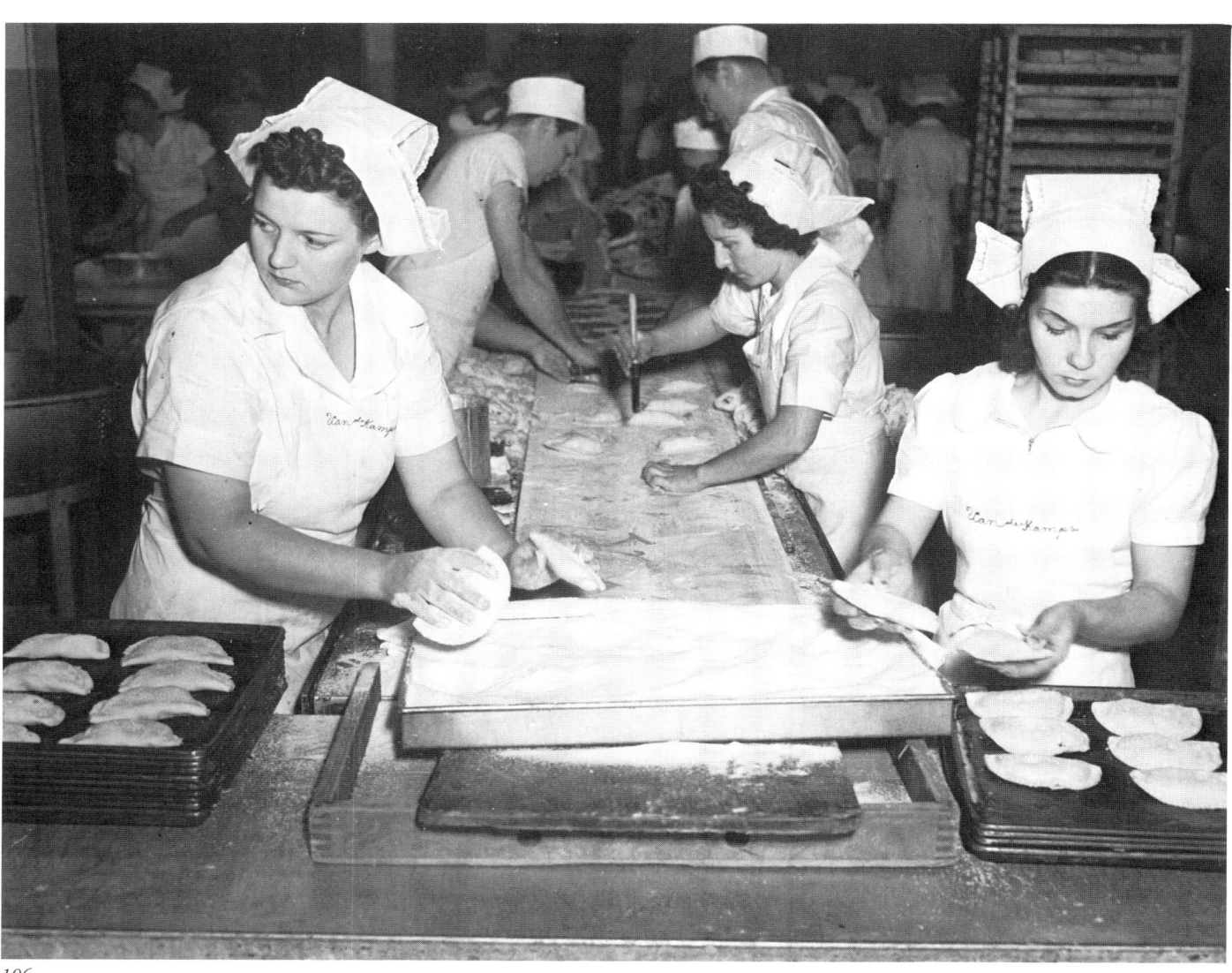

The Jonathan Club dates to 1895, when it was founded as a marching society whose members turned out for political parades and ceremonies. Its members helped elect William McKinley in 1896.

The club's first president was George Alexander, who later became mayor of Los Angeles. Henry Huntington, president of the Pacific Electric and, later, Los Angeles Railway networks, also served as the club's president for 12 years.

It was in 1925 that the club's headquarters building on South Figueroa Street was built. It was designed by the architectural firm of Schultze and Weaver, who had just completed the Los Angeles Biltmore Hotel. Giovanni B. Smeraldi, a famed artist who had worked on Grand Central Station in New York, designed the Jonathan Club's ceilings and various ornamental features.

Today's Jonathan Club boasts some 3,400 members who can avail themselves of the club's many facilities, including hotel and resident rooms, dining room, pool and various shops. Since the 1930s, an added feature has been the Jonathan Beach Club in Santa Monica, which offers all the amenities of a seaside resort. *[90, 91]*

Curries is best remembered as home of the "mile-high" ice cream cone. It began in Long Beach in the 1930s, then merged with Coast Ice Cream during World War II. Later, it was sold to a succession of owners including Arden Farms, Good Humor Ice Cream and the Wilshire Dairy. Curries ceased operation in the 1960s. There were once over 100 stores. *[93]*

The Los Angeles Theatre opened on January 30, 1931, with Charles Chaplin's *City Lights* and a stage show featuring Carlton Kelsey conducting the orchestra. It was built by E.L. Gumbiner, who had earlier built the Tower Theatre, and it was conceived by him to be the equivalent to the lavish Fox in San Francisco. Designed by S. Charles Lee, it had custom-designed furnishings, a seating capacity of 2,190 on three levels, and several innovations. To help guide latecomers to their seats, there were tubes of pale-blue neon on either side of the aisles. There was also a television-like screen in the main lounge which relayed the movie by way of an elaborate prism system from the projection booth.

Despite the amenities, the theatre was a financial disappointment. Because only the studio-owned theatre circuits could book the first-run movies, the Los Angeles, which was independent, ended up playing B pictures on double bills.

Now under the management of Metropolitan Theatres, it thrives by serving a large Spanish-speaking audience. *[97-100]*

Studebaker was preeminent not only in automobiles but in horse-drawn carriages in the days before internal combustion.

The plant, at 4530 Loma Vista, was built for and leased to Studebaker in March 1937 by the Central Manufacturing District, now the Santa Fe Land Improvement Co. (part of the Santa Fe Railway).

Despite a brief surge in the post-World War II auto market with an advanced and eye-catching body style, Studebaker encountered increasing difficulties in the marketplace which not even a "merger" with Packard could correct. Production of autos at the Vernon plant ceased in 1956.

The building continued in use by other companies, which included Food Giant markets and International Paper. Since 1967 it has been occupied by the St. Regis Paper Co.

Where once sedans and coupes rolled off an assembly line, grocery bags are now produced. *[102]*

Cooperatives were formed by California farmers to help turn agricultural production into an efficient business. This was especially urgent before the turn of the century, when the logistics of shipping fresh produce to the east were formidable. Cooperatives established packing houses and centralized distribution points; they handled the advertising and marketing of their products (and invented brand names like "Sun-Maid" and "Sunsweet"); in some cases, they owned their own railroad cars; they also supplied members with farming tools and supplies. In other cases, they created a market where none existed—particularly for such items as raisins and avocados. Most importantly, their efforts helped to make California produce widely available—a feat that significantly altered the eating habits of Americans.

The largest and most efficient was the California Fruit Growers Exchange, which was formed in Los Angeles on April 4, 1893.

In 1908, it introduced the Sunkist label during a famous promotional campaign in Iowa which advertised ''Oranges for health—California for wealth.''

By 1938, the Exchange was operating more than 200 packing houses in Southern California and distributing some 75 percent of the California citrus crop. [104]

The first product was potato chips, not bread, but an inspired decision to link the Dutch name Van de Kamp with a store shaped like a Holland windmill turned a family business into one of the best-known West Coast names in retail baking.

Around 1908, Lawrence L. Frank made and sold a nut-and-raisin candy in Milwaukee called ''Darling Henrietta's Nutty Mixture'' after Henrietta Van de Kamp, Frank's bride-to-be. Then Frank moved to Los Angeles and joined with his new brother-in-law, Theodore Van de Kamp, in a potato chip business.

Their first retail store opened on January 6, 1915, in downtown Los Angeles at 236 South Spring Street. The potato chips were actually made by Lawrence's brother Ralph at another location, but the eight-foot-wide shop featured an oilcloth-covered chute down which the chips tumbled in full view of the buying public.

''We didn't make them . . . but people thought they were being fried fresh in back,'' Frank recalled with a smile years afterward.

It was Henrietta who designed the Dutch blue uniforms and white hats which the salesladies in the tiny shop wore, and which became the hallmark of the many Van de Kamp's outlets thereafter. By the end of 1915, Lawrence and Theodore had established four Van de Kamp's Saratoga Chips shops.

Just before World War I, a shortage of potatoes encouraged the partners to sell additional products. The first was a coconut macaroon, especially made for them in the shape of an ''S'' and it was the first bakery item sold under the label ''Van de Kamp's.'' Then followed pretzels—cookies—and a corporate reorganization into the T.J. Van de Kamp Co. for the purpose of producing bakery products.

The first exclusively retail Van de Kamp bakery was opened in 1917 at 246 South Spring Street, a few doors from the original potato chip store. Only a year later the bakery had to be moved to larger quarters at 257 Werdin Place, while new retail outlets were opened in the Los Angeles area and the company name was changed to ''Van de Kamp's Holland Dutch Bakers''—still the name today.

The year 1919 brought another dimension to the enterprise: the coffee shop or ''bakery lunch'' as it was then called. This first ''restaurant,'' at 126 W. Fifth St., downtown Los Angeles, featured glass-display counters, an innovation which has been commonplace in coffee shops ever since.

But the biggest milestone was on October 8, 1921, when Frank and Van de Kamp opened their first ''windmill'' store at Beverly and Western. This spectacular piece of outdoor advertising was designed and built by Harry Oliver, a set designer at the Willetts studio in Culver City. (Oliver also designed the Tam o' Shanter Inn on Los Feliz, the first ''theme'' restaurant. Owned by the same families, it was never corporately connected with Van de Kamp's. Instead the Tam o' Shanter Inn evolved into Lawry's Foods, Inc., and is known today as the Great Scot Restaurant.)

By 1929 Van de Kamp's had 95 bakery outlets throughout Los Angeles County. A Seattle bakery was purchased, and in 1931 the main plant and headquarters at San Fernando Road and Fletcher Drive was built. Two years later, the company began shifting from free-standing bakeries to departments in supermarkets; ''bakery lunches'' became large coffee shops and within a span of 35 years Frank and Van de Kamp had created a business with more than 2,000 employees, two baking plants, 185 stores, two coffee shops and a drive-in.

Due to illness in both families, the enterprise was sold in 1956 to General Baking Company of Connecticut. Theodore Van de Kamp died that year; Frank in 1970.

The bakery has since returned to local control, but the frozen foods division has remained a part of General Baking Company. [105, 106]

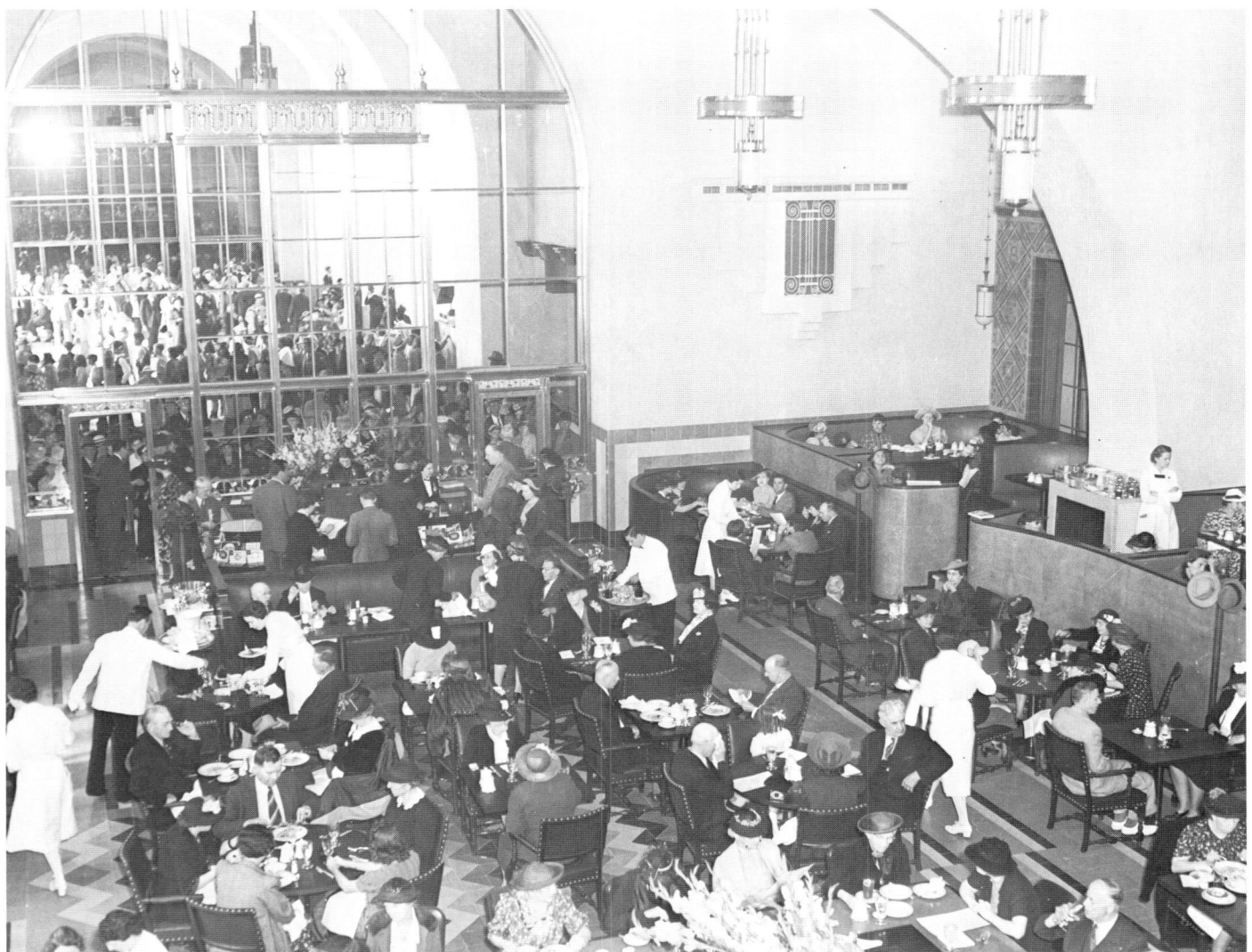

107.   *Fred Harvey Restaurant; Los Angeles Union Station*

GILMORE OIL:

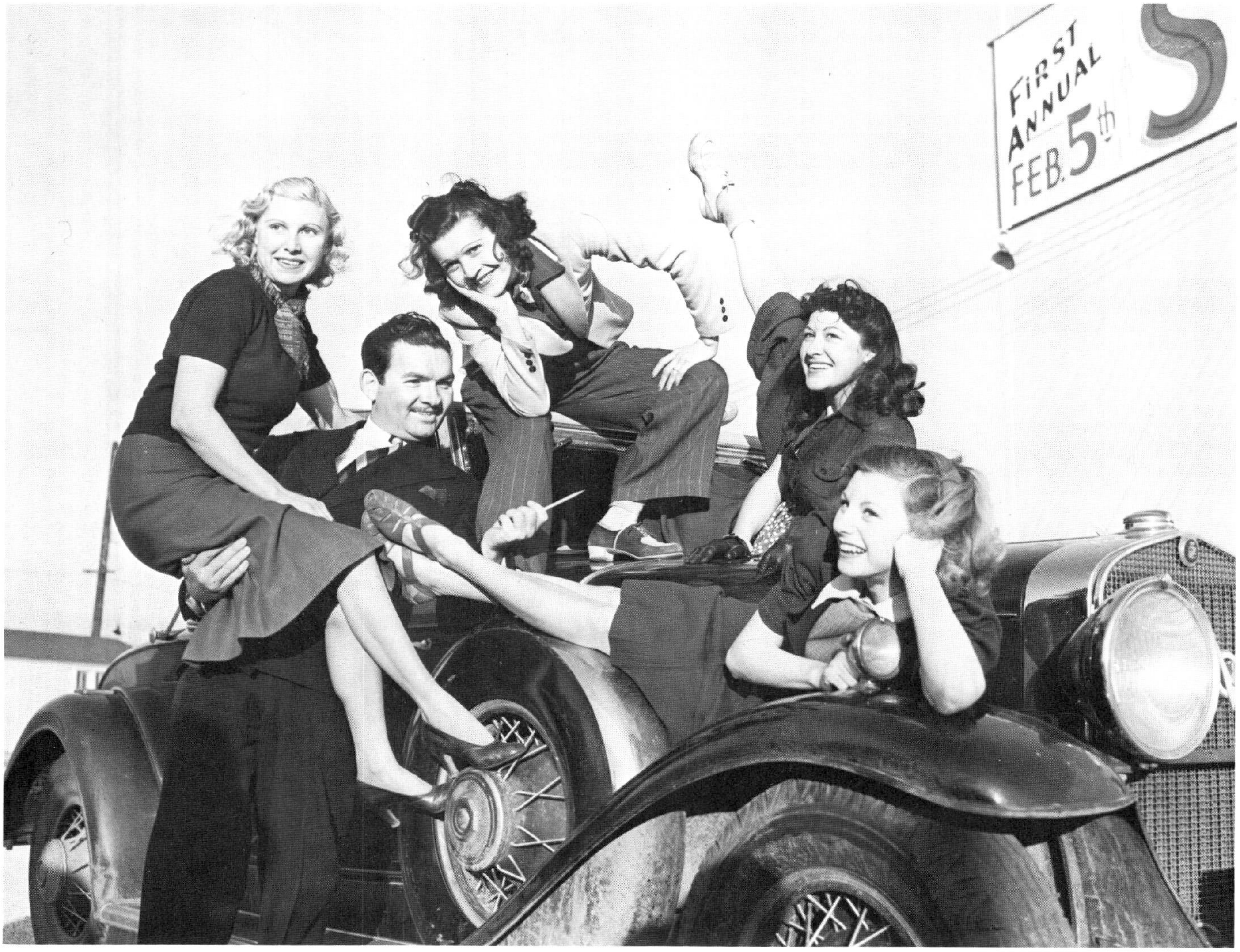

108.

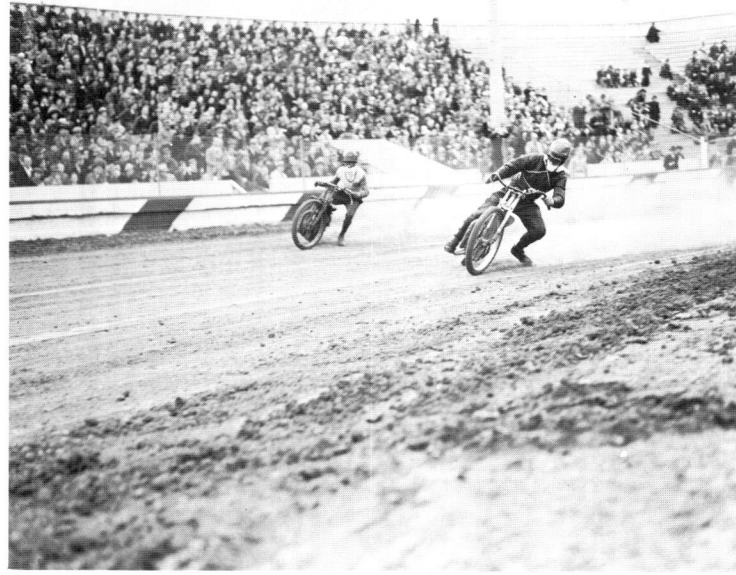

109. *Stunt racing at Gilmore Stadium*

Douglas DC-3 at Union Air Terminal, Burbank

FOREST LAWN:

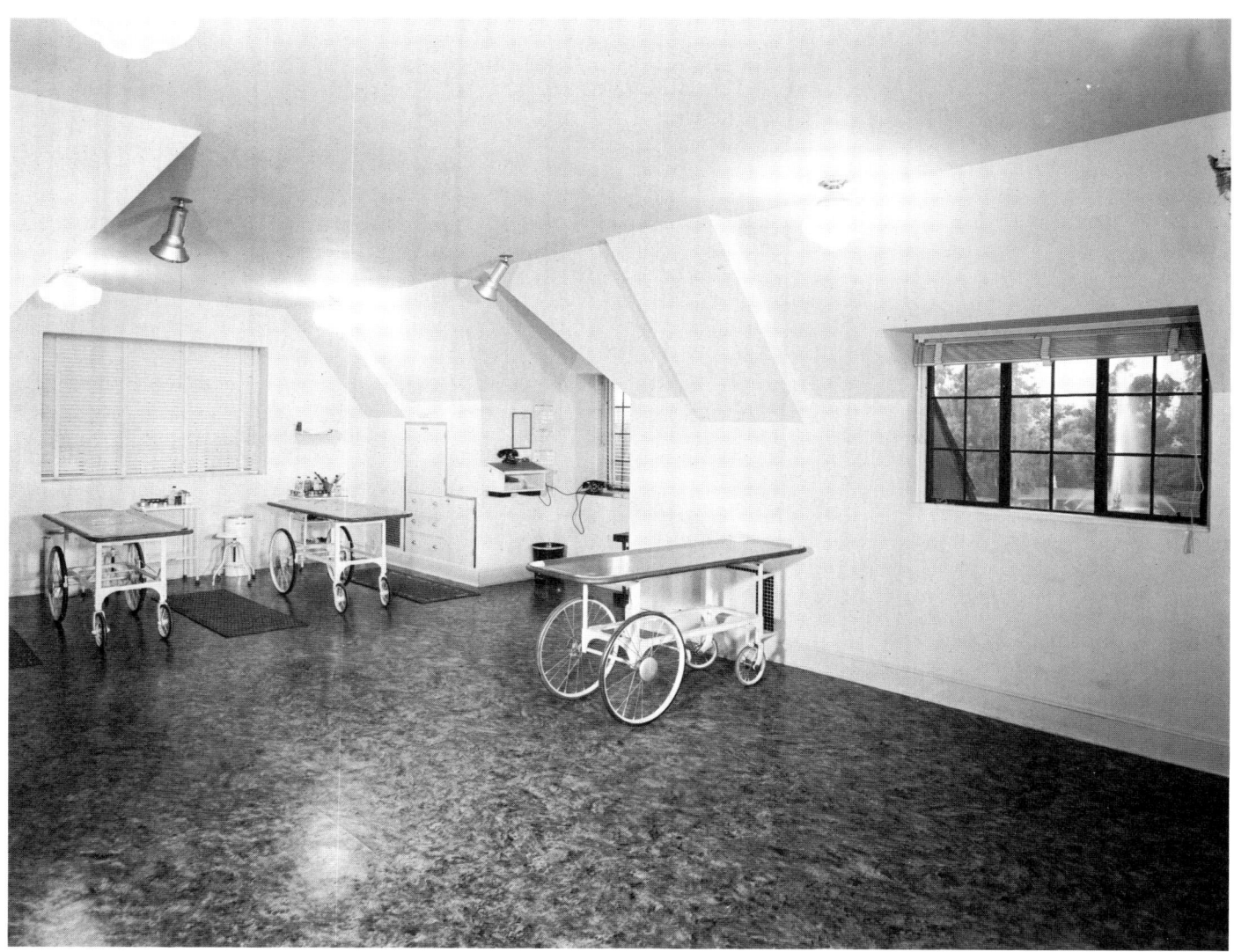

111.

Gilmore "Red Lion" gasoline stations—"The Monarch of All"—served many places along the Pacific Coast until the 1940s. Today, Gilmore memorabilia such as gas pumps and signs are greatly prized by collectors.

The Arthur Fremont Gilmore family moved to California from Illinois in the 1880s and established a dairy farm near what is today the intersection of 3rd and Fairfax. When oil was discovered on the property in the early 1920s, the Gilmore Oil Company was formed—largely due to the efforts of Gilmore's son, Earl (born in 1887). Possessing a flair for publicity, Earl created the dynamic image so revered by collectors and racing enthusiasts. The company used a lion for its logo and was a frequent sponsor of racing cars and racing events. It introduced the Gilmore Economy Run in 1936, the predecessor to the Mobil Economy Run. These efforts were augmented by several establishments built on family property by the Gilmores: the Farmer's Market (1934), Gilmore Stadium (1934), the site of midget auto racing and stunt shows, and Gilmore Field (1938), the home of the Hollywood Stars baseball team.

In the 1940s, the oil company operations were sold to Socony-Vacuum Oil Company, and the stations became outlets for Mobil products. The stadium and field were torn down in the early 1950s when that portion of the property was sold to CBS for Television City. (Lumber from the field was used for expansion at the Farmer's Market.)

Earl B. Gilmore passed away in 1964. The family company, the A.F. Gilmore Company, continues in business today as the owner and operator of the Farmer's Market. [108, 109]

Union Air Terminal came as a result of a drive by the Burbank Chamber of Commerce for an airport. A terminal building and an oiled landing strip, built by United Aircraft and Transport Corporation, were dedicated on Memorial Day, 1930, with an all-day celebration and air show. Two regular air carriers, Western Air Transport and American Airlines, moved from Alhambra Airport in 1931 to make the field their Los Angeles area base. United Airports of California purchased the field in 1934; they gave it the name, Union Air Terminal, expanded the services and improved the runway. By the late 1930s, it had replaced Grand Central as the area's major air gateway. In 1940 it was sold again, to Lockheed Aircraft Company, which maintained ownership until 1979. Now known as Burbank Airport, it is the property of the cities of Burbank, Glendale and Pasadena. [110]

With Forest Lawn, Dr. Hubert Eaton hoped to create a cemetery that was more than just a cemetery. He felt that it should be a place that was just as attractive to lovers and picnickers as to mourners at a funeral. He wrote a Builder's Creed which includes: "I therefore know the cemeteries of today are wrong because they depict an end, not a beginning." Toward his goal, he called Forest Lawn not a cemetery but a Memorial Park. He banned tombstones—"because they are ugly"—and artificial flowers. He built chapels and several imposing structures to house, among other things, specially commissioned works of art, including a huge diorama of the Last Supper. Most noticeably, he had the grounds landscaped to look like a city park. As a result of his efforts, Forest Lawn became one of the major tourist attractions in Southern California. Its success, moreover, encouraged expansion. Today, there are additional Forest Lawns in the Hollywood Hills, Cypress and West Covina.

Eaton brought other innovations to his Memorial Park. He introduced California's first prepaid —"Before Need"—burial plan. He also implemented an idea that had begun in Europe, that is, of bringing all burial services—mortuary, cremation, cemetery and mausoleum—under one management.

Born in Liberty, Missouri, in 1891, Hubert Eaton came to California in 1912. He developed Forest Lawn from a struggling 55-acre cemetery in the small town of Tropico, now part of Glendale. The Forest Lawn Corporation was incorporated in Nevada in 1930. [111]

1940–1941

SPARKLETTS ARTESIAN WATER COMPANY:

112.

113.

WALTER H. LEIMERT COMPANY:

114.   *Pouring curbs at "Beverlywood"; a tract bounded by Hillcrest Country Club, Robertson Boulevard, Cattaragus and Airdrome Streets.*

MID-CITY CUT RATE DRUG STORE:

115.   3773 South Western Avenue

CBS:

Studio "A"

117.   *Radio drama in Studio 1 with Howard McNear and Charlie Long (in the hat), and Ralph Scott directing the Wilbur Hatch Orchestra*

PRENTISS MOORE (Publicity Specialist):

118.

VULTEE AIRCRAFT:

Assembling the Basic Trainer, BT-15; Downey

CURTISS-WRIGHT INSTITUTE:

Flying cadets and mechanics; Grand Central Airport, Glendale

FOREMAN & CLARK:

122.   *7th and Hill Streets*

DON LEE TELEVISION:

Atop Mount Lee

124.

125.

Although Los Angeles has long enjoyed an assured supply of city water from the Owens Valley, this supply has not been without problems. Thus, bottled water has played an important part in quenching the thirst of Angelenos. One such problem with the city's water supply back in the 1920s helped touch off the success of the Sparkletts Drinking Water Corp.

In June 1925, Glen Bollinger, Burton N. Arnds, Sr., and Arthur L. Washburne formed the original company after Arnds found a plot of land near Eagle Rock which had a clear, flowing artesian well. The trio raised $34,000 and built a plant at 4500 York Blvd., Los Angeles, to bottle the water.

Even before they could really get organized, nature took a hand. A cloudburst in the Owens Valley broke the famed aqueduct linking the area to Los Angeles, flooded the reservoirs with mud and filled Los Angeles city mains with undrinkable water. It was a good time to start a bottled-water business, but Sparkletts had not one bottle to put it in, nor one truck with which to deliver it.

Nevertheless, people showed up at Sparkletts' doors with their own boilers, pots and jars. Much of the water was given away free at first, but total sales in 1925, the firm's first year, were 9,500 bottles. A fleet of trucks was quickly acquired, and volume grew to 200,000 five-gallon bottles in 1926. It reached 1,592,000 bottles in 1929.

Although the compay tried selling root beer and other soft drinks at one time, basically only one product has been offered: water. Today, five bottling plants are operated and the company serves all of Southern California and Southern Nevada. In March 1964 ownership passed from the Arnds and Bollinger families to Foremost Dairies, now Foremost–McKesson, Inc., of San Francisco. *[112, 113]*

Mid-City Cut Rate Drug Stores, Inc., was a small chain in the 1940s. In addition to the store at 3773 S. Western Avenue shown in Whittington's picture, there were outlets in Montebello and Highland Park. *[115]*

The Columbia Broadcasting System bought station KNX in 1936, and in the following year broke ground at Sunset and Gower for the new $2 million radio studio complex. On April 30, 1938, Columbia Square, designed by noted architect William Lescase, was dedicated with an all-day celebration.

From this building some of the nation's most memorable radio programs were broadcast. Long lines of spectators extending around the forecourt before and during World War II were a familiar sight. For nighttime variety hours, Columbia Square offered Studio A, seating some 1,200 .

Inevitably, television and changing times put an end to the big radio shows. Studio A was turned over to Columbia Records and the lines of fans on Sunset Blvd. were no more. Today, Columbia Square is still a very busy place, housing the KNX radio all-news operation, plus the television facilities of KNXT, both still owned by CBS. *[116, 117]*

A graduate of the Throop Technical Institute (later Cal Tech), Gerald "Jerry" Vultee worked for a time at Douglas Aircraft, the Ford Motor Company, and Lockheed where he rose to become chief engineer in 1929. Following a layoff due to the Depression, he taught briefly at the Curtiss-Wright Institute; then, in 1932, he enlisted the support of auto builder E.L. Cord to develop a single-engine, eight-passenger transport plane.

With Cord's financial help, he organized the Airplane Development Corporation in Glendale to build and market the plane, called the V-1. Vultee succeeded in selling ten of the new planes to American Airways (later American Airlines); other airlines, however, had little use for it in 1932. So Vultee converted his design into an attack bomber, the V-11. By 1936 the plane was selling so well—customers included the air forces of Turkey, Brazil and Russia—that the company, now the Vultee Division, Aviation Manufacturing Corporation, moved to larger quarters in Downey.

Hoping to sell the plane to the U.S. Army Air

Corps, Vultee flew one to Washington in 1938 armed with the plans for a modified version. On the return trip, the craft encountered a snowstorm above Mt. Wilson. The plane crashed and Vultee was killed.

The company floundered briefly until a new chief engineer was hired to turn it around. The first success was an order for 300 basic trainers—the BT-13—for the Army in 1939. Eventually, more than 11,000 of the BT-13s were sold. From that design, Vultee moved on to develop a dive bomber called the Vengeance (A-31 and A-35). For that plane, more than $90 million in orders were received in 1940 and 1941.

After the War, Vultee Aircraft became a subsidiary of General Dynamics. The plant in Downey was sold to North American Aviation. [120]

Foreman and Clark was a chain of men's clothing stores. Its store in downtown Los Angeles was at 7th and Hill Streets; nine other stores were operated in such places as Hollywood, Long Beach, San Diego and San Francisco. At all but one place, the stores were located one flight up from street level; shoppers were asked to "Walk up and save." The one outlet at street level was in Huntington Park, and in 1981, it is the only one that still exists.

The company was established in Los Angeles in 1909. [122]

Like Jack Maddux and Earle C. Anthony, Don Lee was a Los Angeles area distributor for prestige automobiles who did pioneering work in an infant industry. From money earned as a Cadillac dealer, Lee became one of the earliest developers of television.

The Don Lee Broadcasting System originated with radio stations KFRC in San Francisco and KHJ in Los Angeles, which Lee purchased in the late 1920s. In 1928 they became affiliated with four other stations comprising the McClatchy group in central California. Until 1936 the Lee-McClatchy "network" carried programs from CBS. In that year, however, McClatchy went its separate way and Don Lee picked up an affiliation with the Mutual Broadcasting System.

The pioneering work in television began in 1930. Lee and his son, Thomas, hired an engineering student at USC, Harry Lubcke, to help develop the equipment for an experimental station. On

May 10, 1931, they transmitted a TV image from one side of the room to the other in their small studio at 7th and Bixel Streets in downtown Los Angeles. A month later, a license to operate the station, W6XAO, was granted by the Federal Radio Commission. By October, the first real TV transmitter was put into use; it allowed a receiver one block from the studio to pick up the signal. Regular telecasting began on December 23, 1931, to a total of five receivers.

By 1939, when commercially produced TV receivers were available—albeit in small quantities—to the public, W6XAO was broadcasting on a regular schedule six days a week. The fare included panel shows, fashion shows, home economics shows and some movies; many of the programs were picked up from the Mutual System.

The hilltop studio and transmitter adjacent to Griffith Park were completed in 1940 (lending to the site the name, Mt. Lee). A year later, the FCC granted a full commercial license to the station (meaning it could sell time to advertisers), but the War delayed full implementation, and the license was not granted until May 1948. By then, W6XAO had introduced its longest running and perhaps best-known program, "Queen for a Day." But it was station KTLA, owned by Paramount Pictures, that actually became the first commercial TV station to operate in Los Angeles—in January 1947. Its chief advantage over independent Don Lee was its access to a major motion picture studio with its reservoir of talent and old films. With Lee's commercial license, the call letters of W6XAO were changed to KTSL, after Thomas S. Lee. The identification was fitting, because it was Thomas who had guided the station's management since its inception, and even more so after his father's death in 1934.

The transmitter and small studio atop Mt. Lee were closed in 1949 and all studio operations were transferred to Mutual's Hollywood studio. Following Thomas' death in 1950, KTSL-TV was sold to General Tire and, later, to CBS who changed the call letters to KNXT. The Don Lee Broadcasting System, however, remained a subsidiary of General Tire for sometime. In 1952, with FCC approval, it took control of Earle C. Anthony's KFI-TV and changed the call letters to KHJ-TV. This still operates on Channel 9 in Los Angeles. [123-125]

1942–1943

B. F. McDONALD COMPANY:

126.   *1248 South Hope Street*

CONSOLIDATED STEEL CORPORATION:

CONSOLIDATED STEEL CORPORATION:

128.

MISSION DRY CORPORATION:

129.

130.   *Making orange soda pop; 1601 East 16th Street*

MAYNARD BOYCE:

131.   *Boarding a streamlined yellow car of the Los Angeles Railway at 7th and Broadway*

HYLAND LABS:

Processing blood plasma

APPAREL ARTS MAGAZINE:

133.

GOODYEAR:

Assembling rubber gas tanks for airplanes

HOFFMAN RADIO:

3761 South Hill Street

137.

138.

The B.F. McDonald Company was a manufacturer of safety hats, gas masks, goggles, respirators and safety appliances. *[126]*

The Consolidated Steel Corporation was formed in 1928 from the consolidation of three iron and steel manufacturers based in Los Angeles. In 1929, it acquired the Gallagher Company, a manufacturer of oil tankers.

With shipyards in Long Beach and Wilmington, the company built cargo and passenger vessels from parts and materials it manufactured at a plant in nearby Maywood. During the War, Consolidated filled a huge government order for Navy frigates. *[127, 128]*

The Mission Dry Corporation was the successor, in 1933, to the California Crushed Fruit Corporation. The latter had been set up by the Sunkist citrus cooperative to manufacture and sell orange juice and other products made from oranges—particularly those of poorer grade. The firm turned what had been "waste" (unused rinds and pulp from the juice operation) into raw material for such items as soft drink concentrate. Mission Dry was marketing, in the 1940s, Mission Orange, Lemon and Grapefruit Juices as well as Mission Dry Orange, a popular drink sold in dark-brown bottles. It is gone now, but at one time there were over 400 franchised bottlers of the product in the U.S. The company's main plant in Vernon once employed 180. *[129, 130]*

Maynard Boyce was an advertising agency specializing in transit ads. *[131]*

The streetcar traveled on the P line, which went out Pico to Rimpau Boulevard, and east along First Street. It was the most heavily traveled line of the Los Angeles Railway.

For most of its life, Hyland Labs has been a division of Baxter–Travenol Laboratories, Inc., a drug manufacturer based in Illinois. During the War, the Los Angeles facility helped to fill a huge demand for blood plasma. *[132]*

Goodyear's rubber gas tanks, called fuel cells, had an inner liner that was impervious to fuel. This was surrounded by a rubber liner, and then, plies of fiber. If hit by antiaircraft bullets, the escaping fuel caused a layer of gum rubber inside the tank wall to swell, sealing the puncture. The concept, still used today for racing vehicles, saved hundreds of lives during World War II.

Goodyear Tire and Rubber, founded in Akron, Ohio, decided to expand into California during the 'teens. A California subsidiary was formed with local capital augmenting the parent company's contribution. A large tract of open land was found on the site of the old Ascot race track, along Central Avenue between Florence and Gage, and construction began in 1919. The plant opened for production in June 1920, and within several years all the open land around the site had been built up. Goodyear's presence encouraged development of the manufacturing district in the southeastern part of the city, and was also an impetus for residential development. In 1928, a peak year for the Goodyear factory, three other leading tire manufacturers opened plants in the Los Angeles area, making it the nation's second largest tire producer.

A unique feature of the Goodyear plant was the tall hangar at the Florence end of the property, which housed the famed advertising blimp. Plant expansion used the acreage that served as the landing field, and the blimp was moved to another mooring location in the late 1950s.

The declining automobile market, whose fortunes were tied to tire production, caused the Los Angeles plant to cease all production in February 1980, and the site was put up for sale. *[134]*

Hoffman Radio is remembered as pioneer in radio and television electronics. In the 1950s it made solar-powered radios and an "easy vision" television set that featured a yellow-tinted screen; it was also an early manufacturer of color TV sets.

The company, formed originally in 1932 under the name Mission Bell Radio Manufacturing Co., was taken over in 1941 by H. Leslie Hoffman. The name was changed two years later. The company by then operated five plants in the area; it produced radio receivers, phonograph radio combinations, portable battery radios and electronic equipment such as scopes and other monitoring devices. It had government contracts during the War. [135, 136]

From the *Los Angeles Times*, October 17, 1943:
"Plans for industrializing Saudi Arabia were announced yesterday by F. A. Davies, president of the California Arabian Standard Oil Company, coincidental with the visit of two of King Ibn Saudi's sons, Their Royal Highnesses Amir Faisel and Amir Khalid.

"Partners in the plan, who won't even wait for the war's end, are King Ibn Saud and the American-owned oil concern.

"Davies said the company has been engaged in the exploration and development of the country's oil fields for the last nine years under a grant from the King giving the company a concession covering a large area in the eastern section of his country. . . .

"Now that World War II battle lines are swinging away from the Middle East, operations are being resumed and considerable quantities of oil are being produced for United Nations military activities. Also resumed is the joint effort of the King and the American company to further the education and welfare of the people of the area. Schools, hospitals, irrigation and agricultural training based on American methods but adapted to Arab life are part of the plan.

"The princes arrived in Los Angeles Saturday; they will go to San Francisco to be Davies' guest.

"Amir Faisel, the second son of the King, is Foreign Minister of Saudi Arabia and Viceroy of the Hedjaz." [137, 138]

1944–1945

UNION RESCUE MISSION:

139.

BULLOCK'S:

140.   "Freedom Parade" on Broadway near 7th Street

VAN DE KAMP'S:

"The Rancho" near Topanga Canyon and Ventura Boulevards, Woodland Hills

VAN DE KAMP'S:

MARLOWE BURNS:

143.   *"Windsor Hills," Westchester*

MARLOWE BURNS:

144.   *Wilshire Boulevard at Highland*

The Union Rescue Mission was formed in 1891 to serve, then as now, the needy and destitute. Its organizer and first superintendent was George Hilton, a Major during the Civil War who had become an evangelist of national renown.

By 1893 the Mission was serving over 500 persons daily from a tent on Main Street. Some of the board of directors then included Charles H. Barker of Barker Brothers, H.G. Wylie, a former associate of the Doheny Oil interests, and Lyman Stewart, the founder and President of Union Oil. The Mission moved to more permanent headquarters in 1903, and to its present address, at 226 South Main Street, in the 1920s.

During World War II, with the number of destitute men down because of the draft, the Victory Service Club, serving men in the armed services, became central to the Mission's activity. The Club included an information booth, check rooms, reading rooms, lounges, canteen services, a barber shop, shower baths and 100 beds. There was also a Christian ministry, with frequent meetings in the main auditorium. In 1943 alone, the Club served some 322,000 men.

The Union Rescue Mission is today among the largest of its kind in the world. [139]

The "Freedom Parade" was one of many staged during the War to help promote the sale of war bonds. [140]

Van de Kamp's bought this 38-acre Rancho and dairy during the War in response to the severe rationing of dairy products by the government. With the property, the bakery could maintain its pre-war production levels; it also could still offer butter and Guernsey milk in its coffee shops.

The Rancho had been purchased from the Brandt family, whose land holdings once extended from the San Fernando Valley to Malibu. (It was, in fact, the Brandts' last piece of property to be sold.)

In 1946, Van de Kamp's sold the Rancho to Warner Brothers—for $800. The bakery bought another ranch in Chino, which was later sold to Bing Crosby.

The Woodland Hills property is now the site of a shopping center. [141, 142]

Fred Marlowe came to Los Angeles real estate from a background in engineering. A graduate of West Point, he received further training at M.I.T., and then surveyed battlefields in Europe during the last year of World War I. After that, he worked with the Southern Pacific to learn railroading; for his training, he did a different job every two weeks for a year and a half, from switching cars at Roseville to clerical work. Following his resignation from the railroad in 1923, he joined with Clifford F. Reed, Inc., a Los Angeles developer. Their first project together was a subdivision in Owensmouth (now Canoga Park). They later developed property in Burbank; in 1928, they built "Hollywood Riviera," a 600-acre tract south of Redondo Beach that still bears that name.

In 1938, Marlowe and Fritz B. Burns formed the Marlowe–Burns Development Company. The firm developed "Windsor Hills" and much of Westchester. It received a big boost from the War with its attendant housing shortage. A 1,000-acre tract purchased one month before Pearl Harbor, for instance, was the scene of much building activity between 1942 and 1944.

Sometime after the War, Marlowe and Burns went their separate ways. In 1981, Marlowe is still active; he recently completed a tract of 250 houses in Fontana. Fritz B. Burns, Inc., moreover, still maintains an office on Wilshire at the site of the "Post War House." [143, 144]

1946

GERMAIN'S:

145.

146.   *Nursery; Van Nuys*

1947

COBERLY FORD:

147.

148.

KAISER COMMUNITY HOMES:

Westchester

WALTER H. LEIMERT COMPANY:

"Beverlywood"

150.

DOUGLAS AIRCRAFT COMPANY:

151.   *Douglas-operated facility at Mines Field under camouflage*

Germain's, a pioneering seed producer, is also one of the oldest firms of any kind in Southern California. It was founded in 1871 by Eugene Germain, a Civil War veteran, as Germain's Fruit and Produce Company, on North Main Street.

Following Germain's death in 1908, a company vice-president and an outside seed expert purchased the business and expanded it into a chain of 16 retail stores and nurseries in California and Arizona. The main outlet was a downtown retail store on Hill Street near 6th, whose design was a prototype of later horticultural and pet supply stores.

Germain's rose breeding department, established in 1945, developed some of the nation's most popular All America Rose Selections award winners, including such varieties as *Chrysler Imperial, Queen Elizabeth, Starfire, Bewitched* and *American Heritage*. The company also introduced such products as "Twist-ems" ties, "Hot Kap" plant protectors, "Filcoat" seed pellets, and "Kolor-Coat" seed packets. During World War II, it promoted Victory gardens and provided special seed packet collections.

As suitable agricultural acreage in Southern California dwindled in the 1950s, the company expanded into the San Joaquin Valley. While executive offices remain in Los Angeles, the agricultural division is now based in Fresno. *[145, 146]*

Coberly Ford was a Lincoln–Mercury dealer in 1947. Founded in 1916 by Joseph E. Coberly, it occupied its 8th Street location from 1938 to 1960. Today, the dealer is at 1900 South Figueroa Street. *[147, 148]*

Kaiser Community Homes was formed by Henry J. Kaiser in 1945 as a partnership with Fritz B. Burns. Responding to the postwar housing shortage, it built more than 10,000 houses in California and Oregon. Based on a single floor plan, the houses were assembled from prefabricated components.

As the name suggests, the intention was to build communities and not just tracts. The largest of these was Panorama City in the San Fernando Valley. *[149]*

Douglas Aircraft began as the Douglas–Davis Company in 1920. Donald W. Douglas was 28 at the time; he had come to Los Angeles with the intention of building airplanes of his own design. Before that, he had received a degree in aeronautical engineering from MIT, and he had worked with aviation pioneer, Glenn Martin, for several years. The formation of the company came about because David B. Davis, a Los Angeles sportsman, wanted an airplane that could carry him on the first nonstop flight across the country.

Under the arrangement, Douglas and a small staff produced the *Cloudster*. On what was to be its record-setting flight, a mechanical problem developed and an emergency landing had to be made in Texas. As a result, Davis lost interest in the project and withdrew his financial support. The *Cloudster,* nevertheless, represented an important milestone. It was the first airplane capable of carrying a load equal to its own weight. It also inspired the design of Douglas' next aircraft, the DT, a torpedo bomber for the U.S. Navy.

For the financing of the airplane, Douglas recruited a new group of investors that included Harry Chandler, publisher of the *Los Angeles Times*. With their support, he moved the company, now Douglas Aircraft, to an abandoned movie studio on Wilshire Boulevard at 24th Street in Santa Monica.

When the first order of three Navy DTs was completed and test-flown, the Navy was so impressed with their performance that it submitted an order for 38 more.

Douglas, in the meantime, had completed another order for the U.S. Army Air Service. Hoping to further demonstrate the feasibility of air travel as well as bring added prestige to American aviation, the Army had contracted for a set of airplanes that could make the first round-the-world flight. Five world cruisers, with names like *Seattle* and *New Orleans,* were completed in 1923. Of the four that attempted the flight, two succeeded, making the 27,000-mile journey in about six months. This early triumph encouraged more growth for Douglas Aircraft which, within only a few years, became spectacular.

In 1928, it moved its operations to Clover Field (also in Santa Monica) where it was to maintain a facility until 1973. There, it launched the first of the Douglas Commercial, or DC, series in the 1930s. Of these, the most successful—and enduring—was the DC-3, which is still flown commercially in some parts of the world. During the War, it supplied a huge number of military planes; still later, it built missiles and jet aircraft. In 1967, it merged with McDonnell Aircraft Company of St. Louis.

The plant at Mines Field was built by the Army Corps of Engineers in the 1930s. It was a U.S. Air Corps facility that Douglas operated until 1962. *[151]*

BIBLIOGRAPHY

Andreeva, Tamara. "Each Employee a Specialist." *The Professional Photographer,* July 1958, pp. 29-58.

Bail, Eli. "Asbury Rapid Transit." *Motor Coach Age,* August/September 1980, pp. 4-5.

_____. "Union Pacific Stage Lines," *Motor Coach Age,* September 1976, pp. 8-9.

Clayton Manufacturing Company. Commemorative publication about the company.

Dyer, Richard L. "Growth and Development of Monterey Park, California, Between 1906 and 1930." Term paper, California State University, Los Angeles, 1976.

Farmer Cooperative Service. *The Sunkist Adventure,* May 1975.

Friedman, Paul D. "Birth of an Airport." *American Aviation Historical Society Journal,* Winter 1978, pp. 285-295.

Germain's. *Agri-Gazette,* 1978.

Hancock, Ralph. *Fabulous Boulevard.* New York: Funk & Wagnalls, 1949.

Hancock, Ralph. *The Forest Lawn Story.* Glendale, California: Angelus Press, Forest Lawn Company, 1964.

Hatfield, David D. *Los Angeles Aeronautics, 1920-1929.* Inglewood, California: Northrop University, 1973.

Hattem, Maurice I. "I.M. Hattem and His Los Angeles Supermarket." *Western States Jewish Historical Quarterly,* April 1979, pp. 243-251.

Henry, Helga B. *Mission on Main.* Los Angeles: Union Rescue Mission, 1955.

Hugh, Allen. *The House of Goodyear.* Cleveland: The Corday & Gross Company, 1949.

Hunt, Rockwell D., ed. *California and Californians.* Los Angeles: Lewis Publishing Company, 1926.

Kaiser Industries Corporation. *The Kaiser Story.* Oakland, 1968.

Kilner, William H.B. *Arthur Letts, A Biography.* Los Angeles: Young and McCallister, 1927.

Los Angeles City Directory. Los Angeles Directory Company, *1928-1940.*

National Cyclopedia of American Biography, Vol. 33 (p. 269). New York: James T. White Company, 1947.

Perry, Caswell and Parcher, Carroll W., ed. *Glendale Area History.* Glendale, California: James W. Anderson.

Pohlmann, John O. "Alphonzo E. Bell: A Biography." *Southern California Historical Quarterly,* "Part I," September 1964, pp. 197-214; "Part II," December 1964, pp. 315-343.

Rae, John B. *Climb to Greatness, the American Aircraft Industry, 1920-1960.* Cambridge, Massachusetts: MIT Press, 1968.

See's Candies. *See-Breeze,* Special Anniversary Issue, 1976.

Street, Richard S. "Marketing California Crops at the Turn of the Century." *Southern California Historical Quarterly,* Fall 1979, pp. 239-245.

Tompkins, Walter A. *Little Giant of Signal Hill.* Englewood Cliffs, New Jersey: Prentice-Hall, 1964.

Walker's Manual of Pacific Coast Securities. San Francisco: Walker's Manual Company, *1929, 1933, 1940, 1947.*

Wilbur, Susan K. "History of Television in Los Angeles, 1931-1952." *Southern California Historical Quarterly,* "Part I," Spring 1978, pp. 59-73; "Part II," Summer 1978, pp. 183-203; "Part III," Fall 1978, pp. 255-282.

Also consulted:

Pamphlets, press releases, clippings and notes furnished by the following:

Bell Brand Foods
The Broadway
Jonathan Club
KNX Radio
Lawry's Foods (for Van de Kamp's)
Los Angeles Yellow Cab Company
Max Factor
McDonnell–Douglas
Pacific Outdoor Advertising
Union Rescue Mission, Los Angeles
Van de Kamp's Holland Dutch Bakers

The clipping file at the American Hall of Aviation History, Northrop University. (Courtesy of David D. Hatfield)

The *Los Angeles Times.*

(References to articles were found at the Sherman Foundation Library, Corona del Mar and at the California History Room of the Los Angeles Public Library.)